How Should Sex Education Be Taught In Schools?

Hal Marcovitz

INCONTROVERSY

ReferencePoint
Press®

San Diego, CA

About the Author

A former journalist, Hal Marcovitz is the author of more than 150 books for young readers. His other titles in the In Controversy series include *Should Smoking Be Banned?* and *How Serious a Problem Is Drug Use in Sports?*

© 2013 ReferencePoint Press, Inc.
Printed in the United States

For more information, contact:
ReferencePoint Press, Inc.
PO Box 27779
San Diego, CA 92198
www.ReferencePointPress.com

Picture credits:
AP Images: 32, 44, 50
© Kevin Fleming/Corbis: 56
© Walter Lockwood/Corbis: 9
© JLP/Jose L. Pelaez/Corbis: 76
© Mark Peterson/Corbis: 66
© Andy Rain/epa/Corbis: 71
Science Photo Library: 13, 30
© Erich Schlegel/Corbis: 31
© Ted Streshinsky/Corbis: 18

LIBRARY OF CONGRESS CATALOGING-IN-PUBLICATION DATA

Marcovitz, Hal.
How should sex education be taught in schools? / by Hal Marcovitz.
  p. cm. -- (In controversy)
Includes bibliographical references and index.
ISBN-13: 978-1-60152-452-2 (hbk. : alk. paper)
ISBN-10: 1-60152-452-8 (hbk. : alk. paper) 1. Sex instruction--United States. 2. Sex instruction for teenagers--United States. 3. Education--Curricula--United States. I. Title.
  HQ57.5.A3M266   2013
  613.90712--dc23
                                                                    2012018024

Contents

Foreword

In 2008, as the US economy and economies worldwide were falling into the worst recession since the Great Depression, most Americans had difficulty comprehending the complexity, magnitude, and scope of what was happening. As is often the case with a complex, controversial issue such as this historic global economic recession, looking at the problem as a whole can be overwhelming and often does not lead to understanding. One way to better comprehend such a large issue or event is to break it into smaller parts. The intricacies of global economic recession may be difficult to understand, but one can gain insight by instead beginning with an individual contributing factor, such as the real estate market. When examined through a narrower lens, complex issues become clearer and easier to evaluate.

This is the idea behind ReferencePoint Press's *In Controversy* series. The series examines the complex, controversial issues of the day by breaking them into smaller pieces. Rather than looking at the stem cell research debate as a whole, a title would examine an important aspect of the debate such as *Is Stem Cell Research Necessary?* or *Is Embryonic Stem Cell Research Ethical?* By studying the central issues of the debate individually, researchers gain a more solid and focused understanding of the topic as a whole.

Each book in the series provides a clear, insightful discussion of the issues, integrating facts and a variety of contrasting opinions for a solid, balanced perspective. Personal accounts and direct quotes from academic and professional experts, advocacy groups, politicians, and others enhance the narrative. Sidebars add depth to the discussion by expanding on important ideas and events. For quick reference, a list of key facts concludes every chapter. Source notes, an annotated organizations list, bibliography, and index provide student researchers with additional tools for papers and class discussion.

The *In Controversy* series also challenges students to think critically about issues, to improve their problem-solving skills, and to sharpen their ability to form educated opinions. As President Barack Obama stated in a March 2009 speech, success in the twenty-first century will not be measurable merely by students' ability to "fill in a bubble on a test but whether they possess 21st century skills like problem-solving and critical thinking and entrepreneurship and creativity." Those who possess these skills will have a strong foundation for whatever lies ahead.

No one can know for certain what sort of world awaits today's students. What we can assume, however, is that those who are inquisitive about a wide range of issues; open-minded to divergent views; aware of bias and opinion; and able to reason, reflect, and reconsider will be best prepared for the future. As the international development organization Oxfam notes, "Today's young people will grow up to be the citizens of the future: but what that future holds for them is uncertain. We can be quite confident, however, that they will be faced with decisions about a wide range of issues on which people have differing, contradictory views. If they are to develop as global citizens all young people should have the opportunity to engage with these controversial issues."

In Controversy helps today's students better prepare for tomorrow. An understanding of the complex issues that drive our world and the ability to think critically about them are essential components of contributing, competing, and succeeding in the twenty-first century.

Does Sex Education in American Schools Need to Be Fixed?

For students in Florida public schools, sex education centers on a single word: *abstinence*. "We're always working to inform a child . . . that by being sexually active they may be saddled into a condition that will guarantee them having difficulty getting a job and graduating from high school,"[1] says Tom Belcuore, director of the Alachua County Health Department.

Alachua County schools are no different from other schools in Florida, where the state legislature has mandated that all sex education programs teach abstinence only. In other words, the primary message taught in Alachua schools is that the best way to avoid unwanted pregnancies and sexually transmitted diseases (STDs) is to have no sex at all. The Alachua School District's sex education policy reads, "Abstinence from sexual activity outside of marriage [is] the expected standard for all school-aged children. . . . Abstinence from sexual activity is a sure way to avoid out-of-wedlock pregnancy; sexually transmitted diseases; and other associated health problems." The policy adds, "Each student has the power to control personal behavior."[2]

> *"Abstinence from sexual activity outside of marriage [is] the expected standard for all school-aged children."*[2]
>
> — Sex education policy of the Alachua County School District.

Despite this strongly worded policy, some students have not gotten the message. In 2012 twenty-five teenage mothers were enrolled in classes in Alachua County schools. Dan Boyd, superintendent of schools in Alachua, defends his district's sex education policy but acknowledges that the schools could probably do more to help young people understand the implications of unprotected sex. "If one child gets pregnant, of course, it could be said we didn't do enough,"[3] says Boyd.

A Different Approach

The problem in Alachua County schools may be that students do not hear about the pitfalls of teenage sex often enough. A 2007 University of Florida study focusing on sex ed in Florida schools found that the average student receives less than two weeks of sex education a year. According to the study, "Even though the vast majority of teachers acknowledged that sexuality education, in some form, took place in their schools, it was most often afforded little time, occurred late in the students' academic career . . . and may not adequately address the realistic needs of students."[4]

Across the country, school officials in Muskegon, Michigan, have taken a far different approach to sex education. In Muskegon, the school board voted to begin teaching sex education to students starting in the fourth grade. Moreover, the curriculum goes beyond lessons in abstinence: in the upper grades, it includes frank discussions of sexual intercourse, contraception, gender issues, and the dangers of STDs. Also, Muskegon has broken with the long-established practice of separating boys and girls into different classes for sex education. For discussions that focus on anatomy, male and female students learn together. Muskegon school administrators believe their program provides information on sex that most students fail to receive at home. "The ideal would be for parents to do their job, but that's not happening," says Muskegon school board member Marian Michalski. "As a result, the kids get nothing but misinformation from each other."[5]

Wide Diversity

Sex education has been a part of American schools since the 1920s. Since those early days, virtually every American school has established some form of sex education, but as the examples of Alachua and Muskegon illustrate, there is a wide diversity from school to school in how the subject is taught. Most courses taught in American schools provide students with basic math and verbal skills that enable them to function in society while also preparing them for careers or further education in colleges or technical schools. But sex education has a much different purpose. Its primary mission is to provide young people with the information they need to avoid unwanted pregnancies as well as STDs—circumstances that could dramatically alter their lives and health. Says Susie Wilson, a psychologist at Rutgers University in New Jersey, "For me, school-based sex education has always been about prevention: the frontline of defense against such costly problems as teen pregnancy, sexually transmitted diseases, and the need for abortion."[6]

> "For me, school-based sex education has always been about prevention: the frontline of defense against such costly problems as teen pregnancy, sexually transmitted diseases, and the need for abortion."[6]
>
> — Susie Wilson, Rutgers University psychologist.

If that is the purpose of sex education, then it could be argued that sex education classes in American schools are in need of a fix. According to a 2010 report by the Centers for Disease Control and Prevention (CDC), Americans between the ages of fifteen and twenty-four represent 25 percent of the sexually active population of America, and yet they contract 50 percent of STD infections.

Moreover, statistics that have been compiled on teen pregnancy indicate that pregnancy rates like those found among Alachua students are common. According to a 2012 CDC report, in 2010 the pregnancy rate for girls between the ages of fifteen and nineteen was thirty-four girls per one thousand, meaning that the pregnancy rate for girls in that age range was 3.4 percent. Clearly, many teenage girls are getting pregnant. Whereas some have chosen to give birth to their babies and either raise them as single mothers or give them up for adoption, others have chosen the option of abortion. However, the CDC did report some good news: teen pregnancy is trending downward. The 2010 rate was 9 percent lower than the 2009 rate, the CDC reported.

Room for Improvement

Even with the downward trend, former surgeon general Joycelyn M. Elders says the statistics clearly indicate that most schools have a lot of work to do in improving the quality of the sex education classes they offer to students. "In America, we are in the midst of a sexual crisis," she says.

> Sexually-transmitted disease, ranging from the serious to the fatal, are a fact of life in high schools and neighborhoods across the country. . . . Despite these facts, and despite parents' overwhelming desire for their children to received detailed sex education at school as well as at home, our society remains unwilling to make sexuality part of a comprehensive health education program in the schools and anxious to the point of hysteria about young people and sex.[7]

Teenagers check the results of a pregnancy test. Whether sex education teaches only abstinence or provides a comprehensive discussion of sexuality and birth control, the goal is the same: preventing teen pregnancy and the spread of sexually transmitted diseases.

Most Americans would seem to agree with Elders. Public opinion polls over the last decade consistently show that a majority of parents want schools to teach sex ed. But how sex education should be taught is the issue that has deeply divided Americans. Should sex education receive the amount of attention that is common in Alachua and other Florida schools? Or should it be treated with a much more comprehensive program, similar to how the subject is addressed in Muskegon? These are the questions that have yet to find definitive answers, even after nearly a century of sex education in American schools.

Facts

- A 2012 study by the Guttmacher Institute, a New York–based organization that tracks trends in American sexual behavior, reported that 18 percent of sexually active girls between the ages of fifteen and seventeen and 24 percent of sexually active boys in that age group have received no sex education in school.

- According to the Florida Health Department, 34 percent of the state's chlamydia cases in 2010 were contracted by people between the ages of thirteen and nineteen. Other STDs contracted in that age group include gonorrhea, making up 29 percent of the cases; syphilis, 9 percent; and acquired immunodeficiency syndrome (AIDS), 25 percent.

What Are the Origins of the Sex Education Controversy?

A century ago most young people in the United States received no formal sex education whatsoever. Or, if they did, it was usually delivered by such "experts" as Thomas Washington Shannon, a lecturer and author of several books on the subject. Shannon's message to young people was, essentially, to refrain from sex until their wedding night—which, he concluded, should occur no earlier than their twenty-fifth birthday. "The primary purpose of sex is that of reproduction," Shannon wrote in his 1913 book, *Guide to Sex Instruction*. "Statistics show that this is man's period of greatest reproductive possibility."[8]

Shannon wrote at least nine books on sex education—all imparting his rather narrow view of the subject, and none based on actual scientific evidence. (Contrary to Shannon's belief, most men are capable of fathering children well into their senior years.) Meanwhile, some reformers attempted to provide a more scientifically based explanation of sex to young people than self-declared experts such as Shannon were able to provide. In 1913 Chicago schools superintendent Ella Flagg Young initiated a citywide sex education curriculum, but it was canceled after one semester when critics charged that teaching young people about sex would prompt them to become promiscuous. "In Chicago and around the country, opposition to sex education in the public schools focused on the possibility that knowledge about sexual physiology, reproduction, and disease would corrupt the morals of youth, either directly or arousing experimentation,"[9] says Stanford University historian Julian B. Carter.

A Taboo Topic

The hostility that greeted Young's sincere effort to provide meaningful sex education to Chicago's young people illustrates that for many years sex was very much a taboo subject. It was not to be discussed openly—even at home—and, certainly, not in school. In 1912 pediatrician Ira Solomon Wile, an advocate for sex education in the schools, observed, "This very important phase of education occupies no place in the schools. This entire subject is for the most part tabooed, as in the average home, because of ignorance of its importance, traditional timidity, and lack of sufficient information as to the best time and methods for imparting the necessary information to the children."[10]

Nevertheless, some advocates believed in sex education and were willing to tap their personal wealth to help make sex ed an acceptable topic for discussion. In 1914 a group of wealthy Americans founded the American Social Hygiene Association (ASHA). For financial assistance, they reached out to philanthropists such as oil tycoon John D. Rockefeller, Sears president Julius Rosenwald, railroad magnate Edward S. Harkness, and steel company president Henry C. Frick.

They considered their primary mission to stop the spread of STDs, which, at the time, were nearing epidemic levels—due mainly to the prostitution trade found in big cities. Gonorrhea was regarded as a particularly serious problem because antibiotic treatments for the disease had not yet been developed. Thus, one of ASHA's first projects was to fund tests for gonorrhea at six hundred clinics and hospitals in New York. In its first year of operation, ASHA paid for nearly sixty thousand gonorrhea tests.

"[Sex] education occupies no place in the schools. This entire subject is for the most part tabooed, as in the average home, because of ignorance."[10]

— Early twentieth-century pediatrician Ira Solomon Wile.

Educating the Troops

Clearly, though, the mission of ASHA was not to pay for medical procedures but to improve the state of sex education in America. During the first few years in which ASHA tackled the problem, efforts were focused not on school students but on members of the military, who were regarded as particularly susceptible to STDs because of the houses of prostitution found near most military bases. ASHA was joined by other groups in its efforts to enhance sex education, among them the Young Men's Christian Association and the Young Men's Hebrew Association. These groups stepped up their efforts as World War I approached and millions of young American men were drafted for service in France—a place where it was believed the lure of prostitution would be particularly tempting.

Sex education was incorporated into the training for American troops, but its emphasis focused on abstinence rather than how to

A false-color transmission electron micrograph reveals the bacteria that cause gonorrhea. Early sex education efforts in the United States targeted members of the military, who were considered at high risk of contracting gonorrhea and other STDs while overseas.

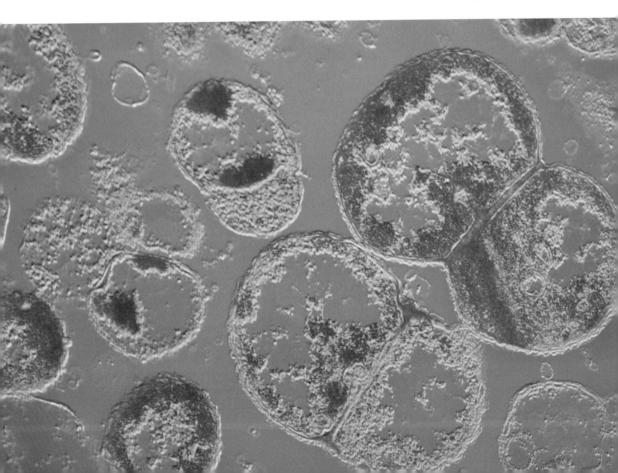

practice safe sex. As part of their training, troops were warned about the dangers of consorting with prostitutes and contracting sexually transmitted diseases, known then as venereal diseases (VD). The lessons were given a patriotic flavor: contracting such a disease, the troops were told, could harm America's war effort as much as being felled by a German bullet. Posters warning against VD were hung in every base. A typical poster—commissioned by ASHA—depicted a soldier and sailor, sitting back to back, each with frustrated looks on their faces. Hovering over them was the image of a sad-faced woman with the initials *USA* stamped onto her shoulder. In the dialogue bubble, she admonished the servicemen, "Boys, your sweetheart, your wife or your parents may never know it if you contract a venereal disease—but I'll know it, and I'll suffer from it."[11]

Though well intentioned, the message often failed to find traction among the troops. During World War I some fifteen thousand American servicemen contracted VD. Finally, to put a halt to the epidemic, the military found it had no choice but to distribute condoms to its fighting men.

Inhibitions Fall

Following the war, the hostility toward sex education in the schools started to abate, due largely to the change in culture in American society during the 1920s. With Prohibition in effect and alcoholic beverages now illegal, the 1920s turned into one decade-long party as Americans drank in secret clubs known as speakeasies, danced until dawn, and often let their inhibitions fall by the wayside. Meanwhile, birth control activist Margaret Sanger was making a case for women to use contraception, arguing that multiple pregnancies and childbirths took a toll on their bodies, affecting their health. Casual sex became a common part of American society during the decade. Educators recognized the trend and pushed for sex education to be introduced in the schools. Moreover, they changed the focus of the lessons from an explanation of the horrors of VD and how to prevent sexually transmitted infections (invariably through abstinence) to frank discussions that centered on sex as a normal part of the human experience.

This change in attitude was fueled not only by the sexual climate of the 1920s but also by the realization by sociologists that many marriages were ending in divorce because of bad sex: many men and women simply did not know how to act in their bedrooms. In 1928 sociologist Benjamin Gruenberg wrote:

> For many years it has become increasingly evident that with vast numbers of men and women the sex life is far from wholesome. The failure of so many marriages, one out of every nine or ten ending in divorce, and many others simply hiding their failure, indicates at least that young people have not been adequately prepared for married life or for the selection of a mate. Another lack of education of youth is indicated by the fact that so many of the men and women one meets every day have one or another extreme attitude toward sex—that is, some are over-delicate, regarding the whole subject as beastly, vile or indecent; while others are actually beastly, and wallow in sex.[12]

The Era of Free Love

Gruenberg and other critics may have recognized that something was terribly wrong with how young people learned about sex, but many educators were still struggling with the best ways to teach it. Whereas some schools turned sex ed classes over to school nurses, others assigned the topic to gym teachers or, for girls, to home economics teachers. In the 1940s the city schools of San Diego, California, assigned topics in sex education to biology, English, home economics, science, social studies, and health teachers. These teachers were expected to not only cover matters relating directly to sexual function but also to respect, love, marriage, race, religion, and family harmony. No matter how schools elected to teach sex education, the overriding message their teachers delivered was centered on abstinence: good boys were expected to respect their girlfriends, and good girls were expected to say "no." As with the warnings issued to the American servicemen prepar-

The Conspiracy of Silence

The notion that sex was not a proper topic for discussion in the schools may have had its roots in the teachings of the seventeenth-century English philosopher John Locke. Locke suggested that the human mind is a *tabula rasa*, a Latin term that means "blank slate." He suggested that people—and, in particular, children—should be encouraged to absorb knowledge from what their senses bring to them. The mind, he said, would then have the chance to grow on its own, developing simple ideas into more complex thoughts.

When it came to sex, educators interpreted Locke's philosophy to mean that children's innocence should not be spoiled by providing them with sexual information. This led to what Alan Soble, a philosophy professor at Drexel University in Philadelphia, has labeled a "conspiracy of silence" among educators when it came to teaching about sex. Essentially, he says, they decided that sex was not a topic to be discussed publicly in a classroom but instead left for parents to address in whatever manner they chose. "Children were expected to learn sexual virtue through direct involvement with their families," says Soble. "Sex was private, and public talk threatened to open it to licentious pursuit for its own sake."

Alan Soble, *Sex from Plato to Paglia: A Philosophical Encyclopedia*. Westport, CT: Greenwood, 2006, pp. 986–87.

ing to leave for France in 1917, that message often fell on deaf ears. According to the National Campaign to Prevent Teen and Unplanned Pregnancy, an advocacy group based in Washington, DC, the number of teenage girls giving birth increased 78 percent between 1940 and 1957.

The 1960s would turn out to be one of the most explosive decades in American history. It was the era of the civil rights movement, the war in Vietnam, massive protests over the war, overt drug use by young people, and explicit content in films and other media. For his 1968 solo album, *Two Virgins*, Beatle John Lennon and his girlfriend, Yoko Ono, posed nude on the cover. And in 1969 the film *Midnight Cowboy* won the Oscar as Best Picture of the Year. The film told the story of a male prostitute, featured nudity, and was rated X—the era's equivalent of NC-17, meaning no one under seventeen would be admitted to the theater.

It was also the decade of "free love," as many young people completely ignored the messages promoting abstinence that were routinely preached in their sex education classes. Instead, promiscuity and casual sex were becoming the norm among young people. In 1967 *Ebony* magazine reporter Charles E. Brown toured the Haight-Ashbury neighborhood of San Francisco—ground zero in the free-love movement—and reported what he saw: "Free love and drugs are easier to come by here. Some, especially the young, seek greater freedom, a chance at life outside the bounds of conventional morality and society's taboos."[13]

Frank Discussions About Sex

Three years prior to the publication of Brown's story, a group of educators founded the Sexuality Information and Education Council of the United States (SIECUS) with the aim of revamping the content of sex ed classes in American schools. Abstinence would still be stressed, but under the SIECUS model students would also be given information on contraception as well as physiology, pregnancy, and STDs. Many schools soon adopted programs based on the SIECUS philosophy.

By 1968 nearly 50 percent of all American schools—public schools as well as private and church-sponsored parochial schools—established sex education classes that included frank discussions of such issues as contraception, the formation of sperm, and the sexual act itself. "Not long ago they'd have hanged me from the nearest telephone pole for what I'm doing,"[14] said Paul W. Cook, superintendent of schools in Anaheim, California, which established a sex education program based on the SIECUS model. Indeed, many school administrators were shocked to learn

The 1960s saw a huge change in American attitudes toward sex, with the Haight-Ashbury neighborhood of San Francisco (pictured) forming the center of the free-love movement. Messages of abstinence were mostly ignored during this time period.

that parents were very supportive of the content of the new classes. In 1965, prior to implementing a so-called comprehensive sex education policy mandated by the Illinois state legislature, the Chicago school system queried thirty-two hundred parents on what they thought of its contents. Only sixteen parents complained.

Moreover, these programs tended to show results. In 1957 the teen birthrate hit a high of ninety-six girls per one thousand between the ages of fifteen and nineteen—meaning that nearly one in ten American girls were likely to become teenage mothers. By 1970 that rate dropped to sixty-eight girls per one thousand, and the rate would continue to drop until 1984, when the teen birthrate fell to fifty girls per one thousand—almost half the rate recorded twenty-seven years earlier. However, in 1985 the teen pregnancy rate started climbing again, reaching a new high of sixty-two girls per one thousand in 1991.

The Political Awakening of the Christian Right

What occurred during the 1970s and 1980s was the political awakening of the Christian right, particularly after the 1973 US Supreme Court decision in the *Roe vs. Wade* case legalizing abortion. Evangelical and other conservative Christians believed the United States was experiencing a moral breakdown. They saw the court decision as yet another symptom of the nation's lax attitudes toward sex, marriage, and childbirth. And they viewed sex education, with its emphasis on contraception, in a similar light.

These groups, among them the Moral Majority headed by the Reverend Jerry Falwell, exerted widespread influence on American government and schools, and once again abstinence became the main theme of sex education class. "A lot of educators have lost contact with the grassroots values and morals of the American public,"[15] Donald S. Godwin, vice president of the Moral Majority, said in 1980.

Members of the Moral Majority and other like-minded groups pressured school boards to cut sex education programs or alter their curricula to eliminate discussions about contraception and emphasize abstinence. In 1981 the Reverend D. James Kennedy, the head of a large Christian school in Fort Lauderdale, Florida, told a reporter, "We do have sex education here—of course we do. But it is presented in a Christian context. That's the difference."[16] And by that, Kennedy meant abstinence, and only abstinence, was the lesson taught in his school's sex education classes.

"We do have sex education here— of course we do. But it is presented in a Christian context."[16]

— The Reverend D. James Kennedy, head of a Christian school in Florida.

Throughout this period, opponents of the Christian right argued vociferously to maintain comprehensive sex education in the schools. Soon they received an unlikely ally when US surgeon general C. Everett Koop stepped forward and advocated that sex education should focus on the use of condoms. Koop held conservative political beliefs and had always been regarded as a champion by

Stoking the Fear of Gonorrhea

Sex educators of the early-twentieth century tried to scare young men and women into abstinence by emphasizing the horrors of sexually transmitted diseases, particularly gonorrhea. Left untreated in men, gonorrhea causes blockage in the urethra, a condition making it painful to pass urine. Untreated gonorrhea in women has a similar effect but can also lead to infertility.

Early pamphlets about gonorrhea emphasized the danger of passing on the infection during sex and producing a fetus afflicted with the disease. A baby born with gonorrhea can develop the eye disease ophthalmia neonatorum, which can lead to blindness. One 1914 pamphlet distributed at clinics to young men pictured a tiny tombstone reading:

> Here lies a little blind baby,
> so afflicted from birth,
> offered up by its father as a
> sacrifice to his pre-marriage sacrilege
> of the sexual relation.

Girls were told their only protection against gonorrhea was abstinence. C.F. Hodge, the author of a 1911 schoolbook on hygiene, wrote, "The appeal to normal healthy motherhood is all-self-sufficient with girls . . . and if only they are given the precautions and relations correctly they will strictly avoid anything which is likely to endanger this function."

Quoted in Julian B. Carter, "Birds, Bees, and Venereal Disease: Toward an Intellectual History of Sex Education," *Journal of the History of Sexuality*, April 2001, pp. 222, 223.

the Christian right, but in 1986 he announced that the potentially fatal sexually transmitted disease, acquired immunodeficiency syndrome (AIDS), had reached epidemic proportions. To prevent the spread of AIDS, Koop urged sexually active teenagers and adults to use condoms. His warnings about AIDS resonated with the American people. In 1987, at the height of the epidemic, condom manufacturers sold 450 million prophylactics. In a speech to students at Liberty University in Virginia—a school headed at the time by Falwell—Koop said, "One of the things that disturbed me most . . . is that my own constituency of [conservative Christians] have been most critical of what I said. I'm sure I stepped on a lot of toes."[17]

Absorbing Lessons from the Media

In the three decades since the controversy erupted over how best to teach young people about the dangers of AIDS, virtually all American middle schools and high schools have established some form of sex education. Many schools remain focused on abstinence, but others employ a broader approach. Nevertheless, as schools struggle with the best ways to teach about sex, a new trend has become evident to educators: students seem less inclined to absorb the lessons they learn in class and more likely to absorb sexual information they glean from the media.

A 2009 study by Children's Hospital of Boston confirmed that when young people view sexually oriented content in the media, they are more likely to start having sex earlier than young people whose viewing habits are more restricted—usually by their parents. "Adult entertainment often deals with issues and challenges that adults face, including the complexities of sexual relationships," says study coauthor David Bickham, a staff scientist in the hospital's Center on Media and Child Health. "Children have neither the life experience nor the brain development to fully differentiate between a reality they are moving toward and a fiction meant solely to entertain. Children learn from the media, and when they watch media with sexual references and innuendos, our research suggests they are more

"Children learn from the media, and when they watch media with sexual references and innuendos, our research suggests they are more likely to engage in sexual activity earlier in life."[18]

— David Bickham, staff scientist at Children's Hospital, Boston.

likely to engage in sexual activity earlier in life."[18]

There is no question that sex is all over the media—particularly in the elements of the media that draw young audiences. Such top pop stars as Robbie Williams, Christina Aguilera, Katy Perry, Usher, Lady Gaga, and Britney Spears have appeared in sexually charged music videos, many featuring partial nudity and simulated sex. Not only do the images depicted in these videos feature sexually liberal content, but the lyrics of the songs are sexual in nature as well. Steven Martino, author of a 2006 study of the sexual content of song lyrics for the California–based research institution Rand Corporation, said some songs send definitive messages about sex to young listeners, particularly that boys should be relentless in their pursuit of sex and that girls should consider themselves sex objects. "We think that really lowers kids' inhibitions and makes them less thoughtful [about sex],"[19] he says. According to the Rand study, teens who listen to songs featuring messages about sex are twice as likely to have sex as teens who prefer other types of music.

Teens and Internet Pornography

Stars like Perry and Lady Gaga may imply they are having sex in their music videos, but anybody with computer access, including teens, can easily find pornography on the Internet and see the real thing. A 2008 study by Pennsylvania State University and the University of New Hampshire found that 93 percent of boys and 62 percent of girls are exposed to pornography on the Internet before they reach the age of eighteen.

Experts have found that Internet pornography affects boys and girls in different ways. According to Dennis Frank, assistant professor of counseling and human services at Roosevelt University in Illinois, boys who frequently watch Internet pornography come to regard girls as sex objects. "[Boys] who do view it and view it on a more regular basis are isolated socially," he says. "They spend a lot of time by themselves, with little parental or family involvement. In these cases, it really does begin impacting their view of sexuality, makes them view women as sex objects and sex as just a physical act without any emotional ties."[20]

As for girls, Michael Castleman, who writes on sexuality issues for the magazine *Psychology Today*, says girls who watch pornography on the Internet often compare their bodies with those of the actresses they see on their computer screens. Citing the findings of a 2011 Swedish study, he says, "Girls [admitted] that they compared their own bodies to those of the women in porn. They expressed insecurity about their bodies, and worried that boys would find them not sexy enough to be adequate sex partners."[21]

Mixed Messages

Elements of the more mainstream media also deliver mixed messages when it comes to sex. For example, the 2007 film *Juno* tells a poignant story about how a sixteen-year-old pregnant girl wrestles with her emotions as she first considers an abortion and then arranges for the adoption of her baby. The film illustrates how teenage pregnancy is not a matter to be taken lightly, but rather one that can require life-altering decisions. In the same year *Juno* was released, the topic of an unplanned pregnancy was given a much lighter touch in the film *Knocked Up*. It was a comedic look at how a young single woman manages to maintain her independence and hip lifestyle in the months leading up to her baby's birth.

Meanwhile, the cable channel MTV, one of the most popular networks among young people, has featured the reality show *16 and Pregnant*, in which cameras follow pregnant teens, showing the hardships they face as young mothers-to-be. However, the network also airs *Jersey Shore*, an enormously popular reality show in which the characters keep no secrets about their promiscuity. In 2012 one of the show's most popular characters, Nicole "Snooki" Polizzi, disclosed that she was pregnant by her boyfriend, Jionni LaValle. In an interview with *Us Weekly*, Polizzi was asked various questions related to infant needs. When asked about breastfeeding, Polizzi responded that babies should be fed four times a day. Learning they require feedings every two hours, she answered, "Oh, wow, that's a lot."[22] Her answers to that question and others illustrate how little she knows about the responsibilities of giving birth and nurturing a young child, which probably makes her no different from other young people who learn they will soon experience parenthood years before they had planned.

Sex Education Is a National Concern

Over the past century sex education has evolved from a matter never discussed in school to one that receives considerable attention from educators. Despite the seriousness with which the topic is now treated, teenage pregnancy and the spread of STDs among young people remains a national concern. In recent years the various media outlets have come to be a dominant factor in the lives of young people. Statistics show young people are paying close attention to what they see in movie theaters and on their television and computer screens as well as what they hear in the lyrics of popular songs. And because the messages broadcast by the media often contain graphic sexual content, it would appear that sex educators must find new and better ways to reach students, providing them with facts about the risks of sex that movies and music videos often fail to provide.

Facts

- **A 1920 study by US government health authorities reported that just 15 percent of American high schools had integrated sex education into their curricula; by 1927 that number had grown to 45 percent.**

- **The first formal training for teachers to lead classes in sex education was probably established in New York City in 1939, when the city's board of education approved a fifteen-week course for teachers who applied for assignment to sex ed classes.**

- **During World War II the American military's strategy for preventing an epidemic of sexually transmitted diseases included distributing 50 million condoms *a month* to the troops.**

- In 1980 the Reverend Jerry Falwell, head of the Moral Majority, campaigned against sex education in schools by mailing flyers to five hundred thousand conservative Christians that included photocopies of pages from a textbook used in many seventh- and ninth-grade classes. The photocopied pages explained such topics as masturbation and homosexuality.

- Of approximately 250 female college students polled, 46 percent based their decisions about sex largely on the actions of the characters Samantha and Miranda in the HBO series *Sex and the City*, according to a 2011 Ohio State University poll.

Should Schools Focus on Abstinence or Safe Sex?

Melanie Lynch teaches sex education at a high school in the town of State College, Pennsylvania. On the wall of her classroom hangs a poster that reads, "Practice Abstinence." "It's my main goal," Lynch says. "But on the other hand, I'm also realistic [enough] to understand that not every single teenager in my class is remaining abstinent. I do provide lessons on birth control, but I point out that they're not 100 percent [guaranteed], and if pregnancy or STDs are something that a teenager feels that they're not ready to handle, then abstinence is their only choice."[23]

Over the years, Lynch says, numerous students have approached her, fearful that they might be pregnant. In many cases, when the tests have indicated the students were not pregnant, she has advised them to use contraception if she suspects the students intend to remain sexually active. "You always want to preach abstinence; that's the most healthy way," she says. "When I first started that's all I preached. Now I've found the balance of how to preach abstinence, but also give information out [about contraception]. I understand that by

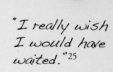

"I really wish I would have waited."[25]

— State College, Pennsylvania, teenage mother Sara Lauck.

giving that out, it's not saying, 'I think it's OK for you to go out and have sex.' I'm just saying that if you're going to do it, use more caution than you are right now."[24]

As a teacher who emphasizes the importance of abstinence yet also advises students how to practice so-called "safe" sex, Lynch finds herself in the middle of a national debate about how to teach sex education. Many sex education classes are similar to the one taught by Lynch—they stress abstinence but also discuss contraception. For many educators as well as others, though, there is only one way to teach sex education and that is to advise students that abstinence is the lone acceptable and effective method to prevent unwanted pregnancies and STDs.

Sara Lauck finds herself in agreement with an abstinence-only policy. A State College student, Lauck gave birth to her daughter, Kayleigh, at the age of seventeen. "If I could take it back and have Kayleigh later, I would, but I wouldn't give her up for anything," says the single mother. "But yeah, I really wish I would have waited."[25]

"Thinking the teen sex problem can be 'covered' with a condom painfully oversimplifies the complexity of teen sexual behavior. Abstinence education has never been more needed."[26]

— Valerie Huber, executive director of the National Abstinence Education Association.

The Abstinence-Only Debate

The debate over whether to stress abstinence-only education or courses that combine an abstinence message with information about contraception has emerged as one of the most hotly contested issues in American society. Most people who advocate abstinence-only education are steadfast in their beliefs that teens should be instructed in their sex education classes to refrain from sex until marriage. Valerie Huber, the executive director of the advocacy group National Abstinence Education Association (NAEA), points out that "thinking the teen sex problem can be 'covered' with a condom painfully oversimplifies the complexity of teen sexual behavior. Abstinence education has never been more needed."[26]

On the other side of the debate stand advocates who believe abstinence-only education does not work because many teens are likely to ignore their lessons and engage in sexual relations with their boyfriends and girlfriends. Therefore, they argue, teens should be urged to abstain from sex but should also be made aware of the availability of contraceptives, how to use them, and their effectiveness in preventing pregnancies and STDs. According to David C. Wiley, president of the American School Health Association and a professor of health education at Texas State University, denying young people valuable information about contraception does them no good. "We are raising generation after generation of sexually illiterate adults,"[27] says Wiley.

Wiley is particularly critical of the strict abstinence-only policy mandated by the state legislature in Texas. He points to young people like Monica, a high school student who was interviewed by the magazine *Texas Monthly*, as proof that abstinence-only programs are largely ineffective. At the time she was interviewed in 2008, Monica was seventeen years old and a sophomore in a Texas high school. By that age Monica should have been a senior, but she was forced to miss considerable class time due to the births of her two children, whom she is raising in her parents' house.

Monica and her nineteen-year-old boyfriend used contraception occasionally, but not every time they had sex. As a result, Monica got pregnant twice. According to Monica, contraceptive use was not part of the sex education curriculum in her school district. Moreover, she says, STDs—and how to prevent them—were given minimal attention. "I got sex ed in school," she told the magazine. "Maybe in the fifth or sixth grade. . . . I learned what gonorrhea and chlamydia look like. The teachers didn't say if there were cures. I think there were some STDs they wouldn't talk about."[28]

"We are raising generation after generation of sexually illiterate adults."[27]

— David C. Wiley, president of the American School Health Association.

Funding Abstinence-Only Education

To leaders of the Texas legislature and other Americans who hold conservative views, the use of contraception by young people symbolizes a breakdown in morality. They believe the availability of condoms and other contraceptives and the information imparted about their use in sex education classes sends the wrong message to students. They suggest that instead of maintaining a moral lifestyle and abstaining from sex prior to marriage, use of contraceptives provides a way for young people to be sexually intimate without fears about unwanted pregnancies or contracting STDs. "Sexual activity without a binding commitment is a dead-end; the consequences [range] from hurt feelings . . . to abortions, pregnancies, and sexually transmitted diseases," says Paul Weyrich, founder of the conservative public-policy institute the Heritage Foundation. "More young Americans need to hear the abstinence message despite what the naysayers may say."[29]

Conservative leaders like Weyrich have persisted in their campaigns to make abstinence-only education the sole form of sex education in American schools. In 1982 they convinced the federal government to start putting its weight behind abstinence-only education. That year Congress provided money for school districts to conduct sex education classes that were specifically focused on the message of abstinence. For schools to win federal grants, teachers could not suggest that condoms or other birth control measures were acceptable alternatives to abstinence. In that first

A doctor demonstrates the use of a condom. Americans are divided on the issue of what to teach teens about sex and sexuality and whether that teaching should include discussions of birth control or focus on abstinence.

year Congress provided a mere $4 million for abstinence-only education, but that number would grow. By 2009 Congress appropriated $110 million for abstinence-only sex education while state governments provided additional funding of approximately $50 million. Much of that hike occurred during the administration of President George W. Bush, who served from January 2001 through January 2009. Between 2004 and 2007, Bush added $38 million per year to abstinence-only education programs.

Two Weeks of Parenthood

Proponents of abstinence-only education stress that the classes offer more than just stern lectures about refraining from sex before marriage. Many of the classes focus on the emotional consequences that often accompany sex between young people—among them the hardships of breaking up with boyfriends and girlfriends with whom they have shared the most intimate of relationships. "Many times the emotional consequences are overlooked," says Lorraine Blanks, director of the organization Sexuality and Family Education, which provides abstinence-only sex education programs in Kansas public schools. "The students need to understand the value of self-respect."[30] Similar topics are covered in many abstinence-only classes. These include the emotional stresses caused by contracting STDs and other explosive issues that arise from teen pregnancy.

Some abstinence-only programs have made use of infant simulators: high-tech dolls assigned to students, who are often paired together as parents. The students must care for the dolls over a period of two weeks, nurturing them by giving the dolls simulated feedings, changing their diapers, putting them to sleep, and playing with them. Essentially, the students must spend two weeks in the role of parents. The dolls are programmed to cry when it is feeding time. To "feed" the babies, students are issued keys they insert in the dolls' mouths. The key remains inserted for the length of a typical feeding. If the student withdraws the key before the feeding is finished, the baby resumes crying.

Moreover, the dolls can be programmed to cry at various times and intensities. The highest level of crying simulates a colicky baby. When a baby is colicky, it feels uncomfortable—a condition frequently caused by trapped gas. The dolls programmed to be colicky cry intensely every two hours—even at night. Students who must take the dolls home may find themselves up at night trying to soothe their unhappy infants—just as real parents do.

The Empathy Belly

Following their two weeks of "parenthood," students usually tell their teachers that they want no part of caring for infants. "We had . . . . [a] doll in my class and after our teacher 'married' us off, we'd take turns caring for it for two weeks," says Richard Arias, a high school student from Los Angeles. "There weren't enough girls in my class, so I ended up having to be a single father. Even for the sake of the class, I knew it wasn't something I wanted to do."[31] David Ruetsch, a sex education teacher from Marcellus High School in New York state, says students who have been assigned the dolls tell him, "I don't want a child at my age."[32]

Another simulator often employed by abstinence-only classes is the Empathy Belly. This device is strapped onto students, including boys, to simulate the physical weight of a fetus as well as the assorted aches and pains that accompany pregnancy. Manufacturers of the device have programmed twenty pregnancy symptoms into the belly that simulate weight gain of up to thirty pounds as well the mechanical feeling of being kicked by the fetus. Moreover, the Empathy Belly enables the student to experience such symptoms as shortness of breath, increased blood pressure, racing pulse, higher body temperature, pressure on the bladder that causes frequent urination, and low backaches. "It's so physical," says Linda Ware, the engineer who designed the Empathy Belly. "The longer [students] wear it, the more they're going to see how their life will change."[33]

Several students at East Coweta High School in Sharpsburg, Georgia, wore the Empathy Belly as part of their sex education classes. "I didn't like the expressions on people's faces," says Rashunda St. George, a sixteen-year-old East Coweta student, who

"I ended up having to be a single father. Even for the sake of the class, I knew it wasn't something I wanted to do."[31]

— Los Angeles high school student Richard Arias, who cared for an infant simulator doll for two weeks.

complained about the pressure on her bladder caused by the device. "And then having people talk to you like you were pregnant for real. I didn't like it at all."[34]

ATM Cards

A Connecticut high school student carries an infant simulator doll (that cries like a real baby) on campus, part of a multiday program to teach teens about the reality of having and caring for a child.

Although baby dolls and belly simulators attempt to show students what it is like to be pregnant and bear responsibility for the care of infants, some abstinence-only programs stress the positive aspects of living child-free until marriage. Some classes distribute so-called ATM, or abstinent till marriage, cards to students. Students are encouraged to carry the cards with them as daily reminders to remain abstinent. Some schools have formed Pure Love Clubs in which students pledge to remain abstinent until marriage. In Lithonia, Georgia, fifteen-year-old Morgan Birch joined a similar club, True Love Waits, and signed a pledge promising to remain abstinent until marriage. "If you sign it, you don't want to break your promise,"[35] she says.

And in St. Louis, Missouri, the Catholic Archdiocese has established a program known as Retreat Evangelization and Prayer (REAP), which allows teens to go online and take "chastity challenges." The REAP website enables young people to post their stories about how they have met the challenges of remaining abstinent. One student, a high school football player named Dan, posted this message: "To me chastity means a lot of things. It means not having sex until you are married and then when you are married not having sex with anyone else but your wife. These are some obvious textbook reasons, but chastity means so much more. I have decided to save myself for marriage."[36]

Some schools have invited celebrities to talk to students about the importance of abstinence. Project Reality, a program based in Glenview, Illinois, that provides abstinence-only classes for schools, has featured Erika Harold, winner of the 2003 Miss America competition, as a speaker who supports the group's programs. Says Project Reality director Libby Gray Macke, "When we bring in somebody like Miss America 2003, and she says, 'Part of the way that I got where I am today is abstaining from sexual activity, drinking, and drugs,' they love it. Teenagers are longing to hear it's OK to be abstinent."[37]

Many students would seem to agree. John Maddrey, a student at Einstein High School in Kensington, Maryland, says he felt uncomfortable in sex education class as the teacher explained the use of condoms. "Had there been an abstinence-only course, I would have taken that," says Maddrey. "To be in a class of people who do think like you think—the way you have been brought up by your family—to get that sense that you're not the only person like that would be a more comfortable environment."[38]

Frank Lessons About Sexuality

A student like Maddrey might experience some uncomfortable moments in Al Vernacchio's sex ed class at Friends' Central School near Philadelphia. Vernacchio, who also teaches English at the private school, teaches a comprehensive sex education course titled Sexuality and Society to high school students.

Male and female students take the class together. Vernacchio

Abstinence Ambassador

Most Americans had their first glimpse of Bristol Palin during the 2008 presidential election when her mother, then–Alaska governor Sarah Palin, was nominated as the Republican Party's candidate for vice president. Later, Bristol Palin emerged as a fan favorite on the television reality show *Dancing with the Stars*, making it to the finals but ultimately finishing in third place.

As Bristol Palin made appearances during the 2008 campaign, it was revealed that the unmarried seventeen-year-old daughter of the candidate was pregnant. After the campaign, she gave birth to a baby boy.

A year after the campaign, Palin agreed to serve as a teen ambassador for the Candie's Foundation. Candie's is an apparel company; the foundation established by company president Neil Cole supports abstinence-only education. "Regardless of what I did personally, I just think abstinence is the only . . . 100 percent foolproof way to prevent pregnancy," says Palin. "I don't see myself as a celebrity; I don't want to be one. But I think using this experience in my life to help others, I think it's a blessing."

Quoted in Sarah Netter, Imaeyen Ibanga, and Kaitlyn Folmer, "Teen Mom Bristol Palin: The New Face of Abstinence," ABC News, May 6, 2009. http://abcnews.go.com.

begins the course with a discussion of values, often focusing on how boys and girls should respect each other's wishes when they date. Sexual orientation is covered in the course—students learn about gay people and their lifestyles and sexuality. Vernacchio also teaches about safe-sex practice—use of condoms and other contraceptives and their effectiveness in preventing pregnancies and STDs. Another topic covered during the class is the emotional stress of engaging in sex as adolescents.

The material in class can get quite graphic. Vernacchio distributes photos of genitals to the students and finds that for many of the students, it is the first time they have seen such images. "It's really a process of desensitizing them to what real genitals look like so they'll be less freaked out by their own and, one day, their partner's," he says. Vernacchio finds that many of the girls, in particular, have never taken the time to examine their own vulvas, and sees looks of surprise on the faces of female students as they learn about their own anatomy. "They have no point of reference for what a normal, healthy vulva looks like, even their own,"[39] he says.

Vernacchio delivers frank lessons about human sexuality, but he does try to keep the conversation light. He often uses baseball metaphors to discuss sexuality. During one class, when Vernacchio asked students to describe a sexual encounter, one boy shouted out, "Grand slam." Vernacchio responded that a grand slam home run may describe the encounter from the boy's point of view, but a girl may have had a different opinion of the experience. "We've talked about how a huge percentage of women aren't orgasming through vaginal intercourse," Vernacchio told the class, "so if that's what you call a home run, there's a lot of women saying, 'OK, but this is not doing it for me.'"[40]

Vernacchio's students respond to what he teaches. One student told a *New York Times* reporter, "Mr. V. takes every question seriously. You never feel like it's the wise sexuality master preaching to the young."[41] Another student told the reporter, "The one thing Mr. V. talked about that made me feel really good was that penis size doesn't matter."[42]

Insignificant Results

Programs such as Sexuality and Society have many boosters among national experts on sex education. Says Tamara Kreinin, director of the United Nations Foundation on Women and Population, "Young people are going to learn about sex and our question has to be where do we want them to learn? From the media? From their friends? Or do we want them to learn from an educated, responsible adult?"[43]

Although many state governments were anxious to obtain the federal aid available for abstinence-only education, others chose instead to provide comprehensive sex education programs in their schools, much like the class taught by Vernacchio. According to the Guttmacher Institute, by 2012 a dozen states required sex education classes to include information on sexual orientation, and twenty states required teachers to discuss contraceptive use.

As for the schools that have remained committed to abstinence-only programs, analysts have questioned their effectiveness, and many have concluded that the abstinence-only philosophy has been largely ineffective. A 2009 study by the National Center for Health Statistics, a division of the CDC, reveals that 40 percent of babies are born to unwed mothers, including teenagers and adults. Opponents of abstinence-only sex education argue that the statistics show many students ignore abstinence-only messages in class and, after leaving school, continue having unprotected sex before marriage.

CDC statistics indicate that after the teen pregnancy rate hit 6.2 percent in 1991, the rate started falling, reaching 4 percent in 2005 as the Bush administration added millions of dollars a year to abstinence-only funding. The rate rose slightly to 4.2 percent in 2007, then dipped to 3.8 percent in 2009. An analysis by the Guttmacher Institute maintains that the statistical rise and drop in the number of teen pregnancies during this period is insignificant and, as such, the numbers fail to show a substantial change in the teen pregnancy rate due to abstinence-only education. "A strong body of research shows that these programs do not work,"[44] says Heather Boonstra, an analyst for the Guttmacher Institute.

Support for Comprehensive Sex Education

Moreover, when the CDC reported in 2012 that the teen pregnancy rate dropped again in 2010 to 3.4 percent, an analysis by the agency suggested the drop was not due to abstinence-only education but, rather to the wider use of condoms and birth control pills by teens. According to the CDC's 2012 report, "Recently released data . . . have shown increased use of contraception at first initiation of sex and use of dual methods of contraception (that is, condoms and hormonal methods) among sexually active female and male teenagers. These trends may have contributed to the recent birth rate declines."[45]

Historical Views of Abstinence

The notion that people should refrain from sexual relations until marriage has a long history, dating back to the era of Hippocrates, the fifth-century BC Greek physician. Hippocrates urged his patients to remain abstinent until marriage and, even after marriage, to refrain from overindulgence in sexual conduct. Hippocrates was of the opinion, long since disproven, that semen and spinal fluid are closely related and that a loss of semen could spark ailments that originate in the spine. He pointed out that young people do not generally suffer from "flux in the back," evidently a chronic backache, which he attributed to their habit of remaining abstinent.

Among those who are believed to have remained chaste their entire lives are Joan of Arc, Queen Elizabeth I, Florence Nightingale, eighteenth-century philosopher Immanuel Kant, author Lewis Carroll, and seventeenth-century mathematician Sir Isaac Newton.

In modern times, some celebrities have been candid about their desire to remain chaste until marriage. Singer Jessica Simpson insists she remained a virgin until her wedding night. So does former NBA star A.C. Green, who claims to have abstained from sex until his marriage at the age of thirty-eight. Asked whether the rumors of his virginity are true, Green responded, "Hey, I know who I am and what I am, and that is a virgin. And with all of the risks associated with sex, I'm surprised you're not."

Quoted in E.M. Craik, "Hippocratic Bodily 'Channels' and Oriental Parallels," *Medical History*, January 2009, p. 105.

Quoted in Steven Novak, "Twelve Famous People Who Were Proud of Their Virginity," Koldcast, June 11, 2010. http://blog.koldcast.tv.

Many students who have been through sex education classes have vouched for the argument that abstinence-only programs are ineffective. Jeff Vautin, a Michigan student whose sex education classes included information on contraception, says the chastity pledges, ATM cards, and similar efforts may be well intentioned, but promises students make in classrooms are often broken outside of school. "It's hard to know at 15 where you are going to be," he says. "I don't know if [abstinence is] something they can really maintain for six or 10 years. Better to be honest to your feelings and very conscious of the decisions you make rather than to say, 'I will not be sexually active.'"[46]

Likewise, Max Mintz, a seventeen-year-old student from Metuchen, New Jersey, says abstinence-only programs assume that young people are too immature to make their own decisions. "Teens given a good education can make good choices," says Mintz. "If they are denied the education, they can't."[47]

New Rules for Sex Education

As the statistics revealed the questionable effectiveness of abstinence-only education, policy makers in Washington, DC, looked again at the sex education regulations on the books. In 2010 the administration of President Barack Obama scaled back federal funding for abstinence-only education—on which Congress had spent some $1.5 billion since the early 1980s. In addition, state governments had spent an additional $400 million for abstinence-only programs.

To obtain federal funding, schools would no longer have to show proof that their sex education courses stress abstinence while ignoring contraception. Instead, to qualify for federal money, the schools must show that their curricula, regardless of content, provide positive impacts on their teen pregnancy and STD problems. The new rules have opened the way for schools to use federal money to stress whatever methods they believe are most effective. This includes abstinence-only messages or a more widespread mix of ideas, including the argument that using contraceptives is a better alternative than no protection at all. Valerie Huber of the NAEA says she is disappointed in the federal government's decision to change direction on abstinence-only education. "We are very concerned that students are not being provided the best health message," she says. "Obviously, there has been a policy change at the federal level, and that certainly has implications at the public school level."[48]

School districts around the country continue to take a variety of paths. Some districts have elected to maintain their abstinence-only education programs where educators as well as parents are convinced that abstaining from sex until marriage is the only sure method to avoid unwanted pregnancies and STDs. Other districts see abstinence-only education as having a limited impact. While stressing that abstinence is always the best policy, these school districts view their teenagers with a bit more skepticism. They believe, like student Jeff Vautin does, that what students promise to do in class is often a lot different from what they do after school, alone with their boyfriends and girlfriends.

Facts

- A 2011 study by the University of Georgia studied sex education programs in forty-eight states. In twenty-one states that maintained strict abstinence-only programs, the teen pregnancy rate was seventy-three per one thousand girls. In nine states that placed the least emphasis on abstinence, the teen pregnancy rate was fifty-nine per one thousand girls.

- In 2001 the administration of New York City mayor Michael Bloomberg ordered all city schools to provide sex education for students in grades six and seven as well as those in grades nine and ten. The Bloomberg administration mandated that all classes include instruction in contraceptive use.

- The University of Pennsylvania reported in 2010 that preteens are more likely to delay sex if they receive abstinence-only education. The researchers studied 662 students in grades six and seven and found that whereas two-thirds of those who received abstinence-only education refrained from sex, only half of those who did not attend abstinence-only classes did not have sex.

- Soon after the Utah state legislature adopted a bill in 2012 mandating abstinence-only education in all Utah schools, a poll by Brigham Young University found that 58 percent of Utah residents favor education about contraceptives in the classroom. The abstinence-only bill was vetoed by Governor Gary Herbert.

Should Schools Teach About Homosexuality?

When David Parker's five-year-old son, Jacob, arrived home from his kindergarten class one day in 2005, Parker found a book in the child's backpack he had not expected to see. The book—*Who's in a Family?*—contains illustrations and stories about diverse families found across America, written in simple text for beginning readers. "A family can be made up in many different ways," the book begins. On the following pages, the story tells how children, siblings, parents, aunts and uncles, and grandparents can all be part of families. The book also includes this description of a family: "Robin's family is made up of her dad, Clifford, her dad's partner, Henry, and Robin's cat, Sissy. Clifford and Henry take turns making dinner for their family."[49]

Parker, who lives in Lexington, Massachusetts, was outraged at the message of the book—that a gay couple could be regarded as a typical American family. "My wife and I have religious beliefs that say to us [homosexuality] is a sin,"[50] Parker says. Parker soon brought his concerns to Lexington schools superintendent Paul Ash, who insisted students need to learn about diverse lifestyles, including homosexuality. "One of the central units in kindergarten is the discussion of families and we show families of all different types,"[51] says Ash.

Parker was not satisfied with the superintendent's response. Parker and his wife, Tonia, eventually joined with another couple,

Schools and Transgender Youths

Transgender people believe they have been born into the wrong bodies: transgender males believe they should have been born as women, and transgender females feel they should have been born as men. According to the National Center for Transgender Equality in Washington, DC, transgender people compose about one-quarter of 1 percent of the American population.

Some transgender youths, as well as older people, wear clothes intended for the opposite gender. In some cases, transgender people have undergone medical procedures to change their genders. Chaz Bono, who gained a measure of fame on the reality television show *Dancing with the Stars*, underwent such a procedure. He was born Chastity Bono, the daughter of pop singers Sonny and Cher Bono, and, as a young girl, often appeared on their 1970s television show.

Some schools have made progress in addressing the needs of transgender youths. In the Miami-Dade County school district in Florida, administrators have encouraged schools to establish unisex bathrooms because transgender youths often feel uncomfortable using the bathrooms established for their gender. Miami-Dade has also trained teachers as "gender safety leaders" who listen to transgender students and respond to their questions. Also, in 2011 the California state legislature adopted a measure mandating that the contributions of transgender individuals to society be incorporated into social studies classes.

Robb and Robin Wirthlin, to file a lawsuit against the Lexington school district. Their goal was to give parents the right to withdraw their children from classes when issues about gay lifestyles are discussed. Over the course of three years, the case made its way through the courts. During that span of time, a series of judges sided with the Lexington schools, finding that lessons about homosexuality are appropriate content for class discussion. Finally, in 2008, the US Supreme Court refused to hear an appeal brought by the Parkers and the Wirthlins, bringing the matter to a close. *Who's in a Family?* would remain a part of kindergarten education in Lexington schools, although not for the Parkers or Wirthlins. The Wirthlins moved out of Lexington, and the Parkers have decided to homeschool their children. Says David Parker, "[Lexington schools] are trying to force their own views, views that are controversial in the adult world, upon young children."[52]

Lessons About Gay Sexuality

Despite the complaints of parents like the Parkers and Wirthlins, Lexington is not the only school district that has decided its sex education curriculum should include information about gay people, their lifestyles, and their sexuality. Other school districts have also incorporated these lessons, and a lot of them go further than simply introducing kindergarteners to the notion that gay households are a normal part of the fabric of American society. In 2004 school administrators in Montgomery County, Maryland, reversed a longtime rule that prohibited teachers from providing any information about gay issues. The old policy even banned teachers from using the word *homosexual* in their classes. That year, the district introduced a new curriculum for eighth- and tenth-grade students that included frank discussions about gay lifestyles and sexuality. The central message conveyed in the classes was that homosexuality is an acceptable lifestyle and should be respected by others. When it was introduced, the course discussed particular religions and how they have shown intolerance to homosexuals. "Our charge starts with educating students," says Betsy Brown, the Montgomery County school administrator who designed the program. "This is part of education."[53]

> "I don't think homosexuality should be taught as something that is natural or the same as heterosexuality."[54]
>
> — Michelle Turner, mother of six children in the Montgomery County, Maryland, school district.

As in Lexington, the school district faced opposition. "I don't think homosexuality should be taught as something that is natural or the same as heterosexuality,"[54] says Michelle Turner, a mother of six children in the Montgomery County school district. Turner and

Boston-area teenagers express their desire for education, understanding, and respect for gay youths and the challenges they face. School districts around the country are wrestling with what to teach when it comes to homosexuality.

other parents who questioned the appropriateness of the Montgomery sex education curriculum were joined in their opposition by conservative groups. These groups argued that the frankness of the material promotes a gay lifestyle rather than simply providing an educational resource about homosexuality. The two groups involved, Citizens for Responsible Curriculum and Parents and Friends of Ex-Gays and Gays, filed a lawsuit against the school district, contending that the course did not adequately instruct students about alternatives to homosexual behavior or that gay sex can spread STDs. "We have the schoolteacher affirming unhealthy behavior,"[55] insisted John Garza, president of Citizens for a Responsible Curriculum. A federal judge agreed with the opponents and, in response, the school district scrapped the program—including the references to the religious faiths that do not show tolerance to gays. Nevertheless, the Montgomery County school district did not drop information about gay sexuality from its sex education curriculum; but eventually, a toned-down curriculum was introduced.

Celebrating Their Self-Discoveries

The Montgomery County curriculum that eventually was adopted helps eighth-grade students understand that, at their age, it may be too early for them to have developed sexual attractions to members of the opposite gender. In other words, just because an eighth-grade boy does not feel attracted to girls, it does not mean he should assume that he is gay. Moreover, the sex education classes for eighth-grade students inform them that if they do eventually regard themselves as gay, they should expect friends and family members to express concerns and doubts. It informs students that they can also expect to experience prejudice. In the tenth-grade classes, students learn about the pressures of "coming out"—in which a student reveals to friends, family members, and others that he or she is gay. They also learn that sexual nature is innate, meaning that people are born gay and are not indoctrinated into homosexuality by other gays. Finally, students learn that gay people should celebrate, and not hide, their self-discoveries. "I don't know how denying information to young people about sexuality or sexual orientation does anything to promote their health and well-being,"[56] says Kevin Jenning, executive director of the New York City–based Gay, Lesbian & Straight Education Network (GLSEN).

Over the years polling has shown that a majority of parents support education about homosexuality in sex education classes. However, support for education about homosexuality among parents and other Americans is a bit more tepid than their support for sex education, in general. According to a 2009 poll by Fox News, 78 percent of Americans believe sex education should be taught in school. However, a somewhat smaller majority—69 percent—believe education about homosexuality has a place in sex education lesson plans.

"I don't know how denying information to young people about sexuality or sexual orientation does anything to promote their health and well-being."[56]

— Kevin Jenning, executive director of the New York City–based Gay, Lesbian & Straight Education Network.

First Sexual Encounters

Additional support for including discussions of homosexuality in sex education classes can be found in studies of sexual behavior among gay youth. A Pennsylvania State University study of

350 gay adolescents found that lesbians typically have their first sexual encounters at the age of sixteen, and gay boys typically experience their first sexual encounters at the age of fourteen. Moreover, a study by Cornell University professor Ritch Savin-Williams found that the average age for boys to begin feeling sexually attracted to other boys is ten, and girls begin discovering their sexual attractions to other girls at the age of twelve.

To gay advocates, these facts provide compelling reasons to include information about homosexual sex in school classrooms. They believe that gay students need to learn about how STDs are spread and the about effectiveness of condoms in preventing their spread. (According to the National Institutes of Health, condoms can cut the likelihood that STDs would be spread from one person to another by up to 92 percent. Nonetheless, condoms fail to prevent STDs if they tear or are worn improperly.)

Many educators believe information about gay sex and lifestyles should be introduced to students at the earliest ages possible. In 2012 a coalition of health and education groups—including the American Association of Health Education, the National Education Association Health Information Network, and the Society of State Leaders of Health and Physical Education—issued a set of guidelines calling on schools to begin talking to students about homosexuality prior to the second grade. Under the new guidelines, the youngest students would learn the proper names for body parts, and by the fifth grade, students would be taught that sexual orientation is "the romantic attraction of an individual to someone of the same gender or different gender."[57]

University of Washington pediatrics professor Cora Collette Breuner argues that it is important to provide children with information about homosexuality before they have the opportunity to develop prejudices on their own. She says, "The data points that trying to cover this stuff when kids have already formulated their own opinions and biases by the time they're in middle school, it's too late."[58]

> "The data points that trying to cover this stuff when kids have already formulated their own opinions and biases by the time they're in middle school, it's too late."[58]
>
> — University of Washington pediatrics professor Cora Collette Breuner.

Ignoring the Needs of Gay Students

In 2010 sixteen-year-old gay student Daniel Sparks appealed to the school board of Cleveland, Ohio, asking board members to include information on homosexuality in the city's sex education program. Sparks told the school board, "[Sex education class] has made me question education as a whole, for while they scared us into understanding what could go wrong, they afforded us no information on how things could go right: On how to protect ourselves, on the effectiveness of contraception, and empowering us with knowledge to make the right decisions before making the wrong ones."[59]

School board members responded to Sparks's request and agreed to form a task force to consider adding information on homosexuality to the sex education curriculum. The school board even appointed Sparks to the task force. A year later, though, Sparks resigned from the task force after concluding that the panel had no interest in changing the curriculum. "I wanted to work with the board to make it better," he says. "No one really wanted to take responsibility to discuss it. . . . After a year of meeting, after a year without a clear direction, the task force decided to retain the status quo. I found it unacceptable."[60]

In response, task force member Donna Marchese says the panel studied the issue for a year and concluded that Cleveland's sex education program, which is abstinence-only, best suits the school district's students. "We researched for a long period of time," Marchese says. "The meetings went on for months and months. We came to the agreement that this abstinence-based program is the best one we can have."[61]

"Don't Say Gay" Bills

Cleveland is not the only place where gay students feel the sex education curriculum fails to serve their needs. Elsewhere, many political leaders have reacted coldly to the notion that gay sexuality should be a subject for public school classes. In 2012 lawmakers in Utah passed a "don't say gay" bill that prohibits discussion of homosexuality in sex education classes while reinforcing the state's commitment to abstinence-only education. Utah state senator Stuart Reid, a supporter of the legislation, argues that explaining

Abstinence-Only Education and Gay Marriage

Gay activists find fault with abstinence-only sex education programs because they are based on the premise that students should not engage in sex until their wedding night. Activists such as Daniel Sparks of Cleveland, Ohio, argue that abstinence-only sex education policies leave gay students wondering how they would fit into the type of lifestyle that is preached to them.

After all, by 2012 few states had recognized the legality of same-sex marriages. Therefore, if abstinence-only sex education emphasizes that students should refrain from sex until their wedding night, what would that mean to a student whose idea of marriage would not be legally recognized?

"The subtle bias is always there," says Martha Kempner, a spokesperson for the Sexuality Information and Education Council of the United States. "They're teaching abstinence until marriage, and if you're a young person who knows you're gay, you also know you're not allowed to get married." Sparks adds, "As a gay student, how can I be expected to uphold a standard of abstinence until marriage when I live in a state where I cannot marry?"

Quoted in Todd Henneman, "Sex, Lies, and Teenagers," *Advocate* (Baton Rouge, LA), August 16, 2005, p. 58.

Quoted in Connie Schultz, "Parma High Schools Teens Make a Request for Real Sex Education," *Cleveland Plain Dealer*, February 24, 2010. www.cleveland.com.

homosexuality and facets of sex in general to young people are topics that are too sensitive to trust to anyone other than parents. Says Reid, "To replace the parent in the school setting, among people who we have no idea what their morals are . . . we turn our children over to them to instruct them in the most sensitive sexual activities in their lives. I think [that] is wrongheaded."[62]

Other lawmakers disagree. Utah state senator Ross Romero argues that few parents take the time to talk about sex to their children. In many cases, he adds, young people do not grow up in two-parent households in which parents are comfortable talking to children of the opposite gender about homosexuality or any other sexual matters. "We've been discussing this as if every child has the benefit of two loving and caring parents who are ready to have a conversation about appropriate sexual activity, and I'm here to tell you that's just not the case,"[63] Romero says. Ultimately Utah's governor, Gary Herbert, agreed with Romero and other opponents and vetoed the "don't say gay" bill.

Other states have also considered "don't say gay" bills. The Tennessee legislature considered such a measure in 2012 but tabled action on the bill after lawmakers feared the law might backfire. The law was intended to eliminate discussion of homosexuality in classes below the ninth grade while emphasizing the importance of maintaining heterosexual lifestyles. However, lawmakers conceded that by emphasizing the importance of heterosexual relationships, the classes might also prompt younger students to begin experimenting with sex at earlier ages. "It's not something that I think is particularly helpful or needed right now,"[64] Tennessee governor Bill Haslam says of the bill.

Victims of Bullying

Opponents of "don't say gay" bills and similar legislative efforts that seek to stifle discussion about homosexuality in sex education classes believe that shielding young people from such information serves only to harden prejudices against gays. Studies have confirmed that gays are widely bullied in American schools. A 2009 study of seven thousand lesbian and gay middle school students by the GLSEN found that nearly 85 percent of the students polled reported that they had been verbally harassed by their classmates. Moreover, 40 percent said they had been physically assaulted. As for students who had come out, 96 percent reported that they had been bullied. "It appears that what has always been a crisis is that much more severe now,"[65] says Daryl Presgrave, communications director for the GLSEN.

Teens in Tennessee protest a proposed "don't say gay" bill. The bill, which was tabled, was intended to eliminate discussion of homosexuality in classes below ninth grade while emphasizing the importance of a heterosexual lifestyle.

Sometimes gay students find they can no longer endure the bullying and, sadly, take their own lives. A 2011 study by Columbia University in New York found that gay people between the ages of fifteen and twenty-four are five times more likely to commit suicide than others in that age group. The researchers found that many of the factors that lead to such suicides can be traced to the experiences of the victims in school.

However, the study found that in schools that have adopted anti-bullying measures and have made homosexuality education a part of their sex ed classes, gay students are more widely accepted and suicide rates are lower. Typically such schools sponsor the establishment of Gay-Straight Alliance (GSA) clubs and similar organizations that enhance understanding of gay issues. According to a GLSEN statement, "Having a Gay Straight Alliance in school was related to more positive experiences for [gay and lesbian] students, including: hearing fewer homophobic remarks, less victimization because of sexual orientation and gender expression, less absenteeism because of safety concerns and a greater sense of belonging to the school community."[66]

Hostility in Minnesota

Some school districts have been slow to embrace those principles. In Minnesota, for example, the Anoka-Hennepin School District north of Minneapolis—the state's largest school district—adopted a policy in the 1990s prohibiting education about homosexuality in its sex education classes because the school board did not believe homosexuality was a valid lifestyle. Moreover, the school board mandated that teachers must remain "neutral" whenever the matter of sexual orientation was brought up by students in the classroom. In other words, they could not answer questions posed by students who were unsure of their own sexual preferences.

In 2011, the school district was sued by six students who claimed the district's restrictions on education about homosexuality made Anoka-Hennepin schools unsafe for gay students. The lawsuit was filed after eight students in the district, which encompasses thirty-eight thousand students, took their lives over a period of two years. Among the eight suicide victims were four students who were gay and had struggled with harassment. The six students who filed the lawsuit claimed they were regularly bullied, both physically and verbally. Moreover, some of the students claimed they were harassed even though they were not gay—in other words, bullies abused them simply on the suspicion they were gay.

To file the lawsuit, the students enlisted the aid of the National Center for Lesbian Rights and the Southern Poverty Law Center (SPLC), two organizations that provide legal aid in civil rights cases. Speaking at a press conference on the day the lawsuit was filed, SPLC attorney Mary Bauer said, "The Anoka-Hennepin School District, where we stand today, has refused to take a stand against harassment and bullying. This policy sends a message to kids that who they are is not OK. Our [clients] have stood up and said 'no more.'"[67]

"We're not asking them to promote [a gay lifestyle]. But if a kid had gay parents, or is gay or lesbian, why can't the school say, 'You're OK.'"[68]

— Jason Backes, the gay father of a student who sued the Anoka-Hennepin School District in Minnesota.

The Controversy Continues

To settle the lawsuit, school administrators agreed to establish anti-bullying programs and to better police troublemakers. Moreover, they rescinded the controversial neutrality policy, enabling teachers to discuss gay issues in their classrooms. Jason Backes, the gay father of one of the students who sued, says, "We're not asking them to promote [a gay lifestyle]. But if a kid had gay parents, or is gay or lesbian, why can't the school say, 'You're OK.'"[68]

But not everyone is happy with the settlement. After the Anoka Middle School permitted establishment of a Gay-Straight Alliance club, Minnesota Family Council spokesperson Barb Anderson said, "GSAs imply that homosexual behavior is acceptable and even cool. Homosexual-friendly books tell students that bisexuality, sexual fluidity and experimentation are OK. Open your eyes, people. Parents, do you really want your children attending a GSA where homosexual behavior is affirmed and celebrated and where children are trained to be advocates for this unhealthy behavior as well as activists for gay rights?"[69]

The reaction by activists like Anderson to the Anoka-Hennepin settlement illustrates that many people remain divided on the issue of whether homosexuality should be addressed in sex education classes. Statistics show that gay adolescents are coming to terms with their own sexuality at earlier ages, and they are coming out at earlier ages as well. And yet lawmakers in places like Utah and Tennessee have made attempts to restrict discussion of gay issues in classrooms. It means that homosexuality is still a divisive issue in American society, and until that changes, its inclusion in sex education classes will continue to elicit controversy.

Facts

- A 2011 study by Columbia University polled thirty thousand Oregon students in the eleventh grade, finding that 20 percent of lesbian and gay students had attempted suicide. Among heterosexual students, the study found the attempted suicide rate was 4 percent.

- Tel Aviv University in Israel found that the average age for coming out has dropped substantially since the 1990s. According to the university's 2011 study, in 1991 lesbians and gays typically waited until the age of twenty-five to tell friends and family members about their sexual identities. By 2010, the study says, that age had dropped to sixteen.

- A 2011 University of Chicago study found that 64 percent of people between the ages of eighteen and twenty-nine support same-sex marriage. People in that age group were likely to have been exposed to information about homosexuality in their high school sex ed classes. For older people—those who are unlikely to have learned about homosexuality in their sex ed classes—support for same-sex marriage declines, with just 37 percent of those over sixty in support of gay marriage.

- A University of Pittsburgh study reported in 2011 that gay youths are three times more likely to miss school than other young people because of fears they will be bullied on school grounds.

Should Schools Do More than Teach About Sex?

By October 2007, Gloucester High School nurse Kim Daly could not help but notice that an unusually large number of girls at the Massachusetts school had asked for pregnancy tests—some more than once. By May 2008, Daly had administered 150 pregnancy tests to Gloucester students, and eighteen of the tests indicated the girls were pregnant. All the pregnant girls were sixteen or younger. One of the pregnant teens was Kyla Brown, who admitted to having unprotected sex with her boyfriend. "We didn't use anything," she shrugged, after Daly broke the news to her. "It was one of those teenage things, like, it won't happen to me."[70]

Gloucester parents and school officials were shocked at the news that eighteen students had gotten pregnant in one year, but they eventually acknowledged that they may have had themselves to blame. The Sexuality Information and Education Council of the United States (SIECUS) and other authorities recommend that schools provide some form of sex education to students from the earliest grades through the senior year of high school. "Comprehensive school-based sexuality education should be a part of the education program at every grade,"[71] SIECUS states. At Gloucester, the school district's sex education classes ended after freshman year.

Gloucester mayor Carolyn Kirk concedes that the community lacked the resources to provide the students with comprehensive sex education through the twelfth grade as well as other programs that may have helped teach values to students. "This is a city in transition going through a hard economic time," she says. "There are cuts in economic programs, cuts in services, cuts in after-school programs, and they're all impacting the social climate. We really let these kids down."[72]

A Controversial Step

In the months following the revelations about the Gloucester pregnancies, school officials made some changes. They extended sex education classes into the upper high school grades and also took the controversial step of making prescription birth control pills and condoms available free for students in the school district's medical clinic. Prior to the school board's action, the nearest place Gloucester girls could anonymously obtain birth control was at a women's health clinic located some 20 miles (32km) from town—a trip most teenage girls were unlikely to make on their own, particularly those too young to drive.

Not everybody agreed with the new Gloucester sex ed policy. A number of parents complained that prophylactics and birth control pills should not be distributed on school grounds, insisting that abstinence-only education should be the preferred course for Gloucester students. "The school [board] listens to what everyone says and then just does what they were going to do all along," says Gloucester parent Glen Bresnahan. "They should be ashamed."[73]

Girls and the Pill

Gloucester's solution to its teen pregnancy crisis—providing birth control pills and condoms to students—is not unique. Many high schools have made birth control available to students for free and with no questions asked.

These schools have concluded that it is necessary to provide contraceptives to students because it became evident to educators that although some students may have found ways to obtain contraceptives on their own, others had not. As for the students

Nowadays, condoms are openly displayed and easy to buy in pharmacies, convenience stores, and supermarkets. This was not always the case. They were once kept behind store counters or in locked cabinets.

who obtained access to contraceptives, it has become obvious that many of them are unsure of how they work.

In 2012 the National Campaign to Prevent Teen Pregnancy reported that 40 percent of teenage girls who responded to a survey said they do not use birth control pills or other methods of contraception because they do not believe they are effective. A study released the same year by the Centers for Disease Control and Prevention (CDC) provided a similar scenario: a third of some five thousand pregnant teens surveyed by the agency said they do not use birth control because they do not believe in the effectiveness of contraception. Says Bill Albert, a spokesperson for the National Campaign to Prevent Teen Pregnancy, "Not to get too biological here, but the only teen girls getting pregnant are the ones who are having sex and not using contraception, carefully, or at all."[74]

Condom Sales Are Restricted

Some teen girls may be unsure of the effectiveness of birth control pills, but statistics show that among teen boys, condom use is becoming more common. A 2012 report by the National Survey of Family Growth, a project of the CDC, found that 80 percent of teenage boys who have sex use condoms. In 2002 a similar survey reported that 72 percent of sexually active teenage boys were condoms users.

Today it is relatively easy for teenagers and most everyone else to obtain condoms. Most pharmacies, convenience stores, and supermarkets have made prophylactics available on publicly displayed racks. That was not always the case, though. Years ago it was not unusual for a teenage boy's condom-buying experience to be one fraught with nervousness and fear. The 1970 film *Summer of '42* well-illustrated this era; the movie featured a scene in which a teenager enters a pharmacy to ask the pharmacist for a box of condoms. The humorous scene is a highlight of the movie, as the teen fumbles his way through a very uncomfortable moment—ordering an ice cream cone, with sprinkles, before blurting out that he would also like to buy prophylactics. And yet the scene was probably very familiar to many of the teenage boys in the audience who knew the embarrassing feeling of trying to buy condoms from frowning pharmacists.

In fact, pharmacies seemed to go out of their way to make it difficult for teenagers—as well as everyone else—to purchase condoms. A 1992 study by the New York City Department of Consumer Affairs (DCA) surveyed 150 pharmacies in the city and found that more than half of the stores kept the condoms behind the counter or in locked displays. "It's both bad health and bad business for drug stores to treat condoms as if they were contraband," said Mark Green, the city's commissioner of consumer affairs. "Much like in the movie *Summer of '42*, where the terrified adolescent had to build up his courage to blurt out a request for a long list of drug store items—only then mumbling the word 'rubbers'—many people are too embarrassed to ask for condoms. But not using a condom in 1992 can have much more serious implications than not using one in 1942."[75]

Condoms in Schools

During a 1997 interview Marcia Spector, the executive director of the Suffolk Network for Adolescent Pregnancy on Long Island, New York, said she often encountered boys who admitted to using plastic kitchen wrap during sex because they were too frightened to walk into pharmacies to buy condoms. "There are kids who will use Saran Wrap because they're too embarrassed to buy a condom and think that Saran Wrap will protect them,"[76] she said. Saran Wrap, Spector pointed out, is not an effective prophylactic.

Both Green and Spector made those comments during the 1990s, a time when public health experts were concerned about the AIDS epidemic and questioned why drug stores were failing to heed the declaration by Surgeon General C. Everett Koop that condom use was the most effective way to prevent the spread of the disease. The New York DCA study showed that pharmacies that placed condoms in easily accessible displays along store aisles sold twice as many prophylactics as stores that kept them locked up or behind the counter.

As Green expressed his frustrations about the condom sales policies of many New York pharmacies, some schools were already developing plans on their own to distribute condoms to their students. In 1985 school officials in Chicago launched a pilot program to distribute condoms at two city high schools. Their aim was to cut down on teen pregnancies—the two schools had the highest teen pregnancy rates in the city. At the time the notion of distributing condoms in the school nurse's office was a radical idea, and many critics voiced objections. The Reverend Arthur M. Brazier, an influential Chicago minister, said the distribution of condoms by school officials would send a signal to teens that premarital sex is acceptable. Brazier questioned why it would be acceptable to distribute condoms in a high school but unacceptable to distribute marijuana in a city school where drug use is a problem. "There's a problem with marijuana," he said. "Are schools going to set up clinics to show kids how to avoid good and bad strains of marijuana?"[77]

Despite the objections of critics like Brazier, school-based condom distribution programs soon spread to other cities—particularly after Koop advised sexually active young people to use condoms as protection against AIDS. In 1986 New York launched a pilot program to provide condoms at nine city high schools. By

1990 all New York City high schools were making condoms available to students. New York high school students welcomed the policy. "Too many girls are getting pregnant, too many diseases are going around," seventeen-year-old Akiba Robinson told a reporter in 1990. "By giving condoms, the school is helping young people who can't ask their parents for condoms or who can't afford to buy them in the store. By dispensing condoms, it means they care about students. They're telling students to protect themselves."[78]

Support and Opposition

Many other school systems followed the lead of Chicago and New York. In 2007 the National Assembly on School-Based Health Care in Washington, DC, reported that some 30 percent of high schools make condoms available to students. About 1 percent also make prescription birth control pills available to girls.

Schools that give condoms and birth control pills to their students are doing so with the blessing of the American Medical Association (AMA), the national organization representing the medical profession, which in 2000 urged schools to adopt contraceptive distribution programs. Subsequent studies have backed the AMA's position. A study cited by the Massachusetts Alliance on Teen Pregnancy found that between 2002 and 2008, the condom distribution program in Holyoke public schools cut sexually transmitted disease cases among adolescent boys by half, from about eight per one thousand boys to about four per one thousand.

But some physicians oppose making condoms available in schools. US senator Tom Coburn of Oklahoma, an obstetrician-gynecologist and member of the AMA, supports abstinence-only programs and insists that policies permitting condom distribution in schools send signals to students that it is permissible to have sex. "I am extremely disappointed in the AMA," says Coburn. "When it comes to sex, [the AMA] does not have the courage, as an institution, to give the best medical advice, which is to be sexually abstinent until you're in a married, monogamous relationship."[79]

"By giving condoms, the school is helping young people who can't ask their parents for condoms or who can't afford to buy them in the store."[78]

— New York City high school student Akiba Robinson.

Distributing Condoms in Middle Schools

Despite the concerns of critics like Coburn, more and more schools have adopted condom distribution policies. Even some middle schools make contraceptives available—perhaps as a reaction to statistics compiled by the Guttmacher Institute revealing that 13 percent of girls and 15 percent of boys report having sex before the age of fifteen. One middle school that elects to provide contraception to students is King Middle School in Portland, Maine, which started making prophylactics available in 2007.

Douglas Gardner, director of the Health and Human Services Department for the city, says the decision was made to make condoms available to students after seventeen King students got pregnant in the space of four years. "These kids are far too young to be sexually active," Gardner says. "You can't argue that any differently. But there is a small group of kids, and thankfully it's a small group, who are reporting that they are sexually active, and we need to do all we can to protect them."[80]

Parents and other residents of Portland are divided on the issue. "It brings home the fact that my 13-year-old daughter has friends and people around her who are sexually active," says Kitty Purington, the mother of a King student. "But at least it's a good alternative in a not-so-good situation. No one is going to stand up and cheer that 12- and 13-year-olds are having sex, but it's not anything new."[81] But Portland political leader Nick McGee says the school's birth control policy sends the wrong message—that sex by middle school students is permitted as long as they use birth control. "It's an attack on the moral fiber of our community, and a black eye for our state,"[82] he says.

> "There is a small group of kids, and thankfully it's a small group, who are reporting that they are sexually active, and we need to do all we can to protect them."[80]
>
> — Douglas Gardner, director of the Health and Human Services Department for Portland, Maine.

Family Planning Clinics

Although some schools have decided not to distribute condoms or birth control pills to their students, they are agreeable to referring students to organizations that will. The Planned Parenthood Federation of America is a national organization that runs eight

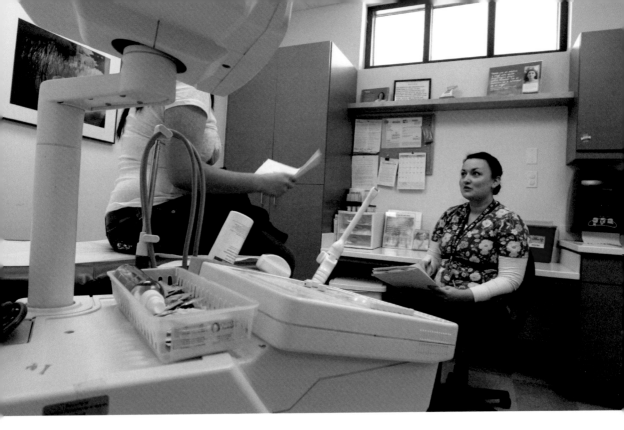

hundred clinics across the country, providing pregnancy tests, Pap tests, breast cancer examinations, and tests for STDs to clients. Some Planned Parenthood clinics provide abortions. In 2011 Planned Parenthood also provided 2.2 million contraceptives to its clients, many of whom are teenage girls.

A similar organization is the Family Planning Councils of America, which sponsors clinics in twenty-one American cities. In addition, many independent groups sponsor free or low-cost women's health clinics that enable teenage girls to obtain birth control pills and other forms of contraception. Among them are the Women's Community Clinic of San Francisco; Life Choices Women's Clinics of Phoenix, Arizona; and the Women's Clinic and Family Counseling Center of Los Angeles. In addition, some local governments and hospitals also provide contraceptive services to clients, either free or at a low cost. A 2011 Guttmacher Institute study reported that adolescents as well as adults can find free or low-cost contraceptive services at more than eight thousand clinics in America.

A clinical assistant talks with a patient at a Planned Parenthood clinic in Austin, Texas. Some school districts that do not distribute birth control to students instead refer them to family planning clinics such as this one, which offers a variety of services.

The Message of *Toothpaste*

When six students—including the school valedictorian—at Mission High School in Mission, Texas, got pregnant, four students felt they needed to make a statement about condom use. In 2005 the four students—Kristal Villarreal, Laura Coria, Gladys Sanchez, and Amanda Ramierez—wrote and produced a film titled *Toothpaste*. The title refers to a code word many teens use to describe condoms.

The film tells the story of two couples, Cristina and Bobby and Carlos and Jennifer, who attend a party. Prior to the party, Cristina and Jennifer buy condoms in a drug store, but at the party Cristina and her boyfriend decide to have sex but do not use a prophylactic—she left the condoms in her purse in another room. Cristina later learns she is pregnant. The film went on to win a national award by Scenarios USA, a New York City group that works with young filmmakers to help address social issues. *Toothpaste* was also aired on the Showtime network and has been purchased by numerous schools for use in their sex education classes. "I guess it has a good message in it," says Robert Cerda, who plays Bobby in the sixteen-minute film. "Be careful about all the decisions you make, all the time, mentally, sexually."

Quoted in Lynn Brezosky, "Teens Film a Frank Lesson on Safe Sex; with Many Peers Having Babies, Four Girls in the Valley Felt It Was Time to Discuss Condoms," *Houston Chronicle*, May 15, 2005, p. 3.

The State College, Pennsylvania, high school where Melanie Lynch teaches sex education does not provide condoms to students, but Lynch will refer students to organizations that do. "One student actually came [to me] and said, 'I'm worried that my girlfriend might be pregnant.' And I talked to him again about birth control and gave him the number for Family Planning."[83]

Outreach to Boys

Some groups do not wait for referrals from schools. Rather, they attempt to provide outreach to students, engaging young people in sex education away from school grounds. In Lane County, Oregon, the local Planned Parenthood chapter has organized REVolution, a youth action council. REVolution, which is composed of students, stages an annual concert featuring local bands. Between performances, members of the student council address the audience about how to make decisions when it comes to sex. "High school students are sexually active," says Emily Rooke, a fifteen-year-old member of the Lane County REVolution council. "The problem is they're really uncomfortable talking about it. It's a hard subject."[84]

A similar program is run by the Planned Parenthood Teen Council in Fremont, Minnesota, near Minneapolis. Lars Hansen, eighteen, a member of the council, speaks before middle school and high school classes about the importance of practicing abstinence and safe sex. Hansen says it did not take him long to realize that teenage boys have a lot to learn about contraception. "All the bone-headed things said [in classrooms] are said by the boys," Hansen says. "That's why I got interested in educating them. The boys weren't serious, and that made me mad."[85]

> "All the bone-headed things said [in classrooms] are said by the boys. That's why I got interested in educating them. The boys weren't serious, and that made me mad."[85]
>
> — Lars Hansen, a member of the Planned Parenthood Teen Council in Fremont, Minnesota.

Educating Their Peers

Hansen is one of many young people who have joined a movement of teens to educate their peers about making the right decisions when it comes to sex. "Society has shunned teen pregnancy for decades, but now we ourselves are starting to realize that protecting against unplanned pregnancy is not only our responsibility but our right,"[86] says Anna Bialek, seventeen, of Princeton, New Jersey.

Bialek is active in the organization Sex, Etc., a program sponsored by Answer, a national sex education project based at Rutgers University in New Jersey. Sex, Etc. maintains a website, www.sexetc.org, and publishes a national magazine, *Sex, Etc.*, which features stories by teen writers that focus on abstinence, safe sex, STDs, homosexuality, and similar topics. The magazine has a circulation of about forty-five thousand and is available on the shelves of many public libraries.

Another Sex, Etc. volunteer is Christine Coleman, who hopes her organization and similar groups will not only influence peers but also sex educators, who she feels can do a better job of providing the information teens need to know about sex. Coleman

Giving Out Condoms—on the Street

Each day at 3:00 p.m. Desmond Grady, a worker at the Fremont Community Health Clinic in Fremont, Minnesota, just north of Minneapolis, leaves the clinic to walk the streets of the town, searching for teenage boys as they leave school. Grady hopes to reach the boys in a casual and relaxed environment rather than in a classroom, which many young people find to be an uncomfortable place to learn about sex.

When Grady approaches the boys, he first offers them free condoms. He quickly follows up the offer with a serious discussion about STDs and unwanted pregnancies, showing them graphic photographs of diseased organs infected with gonorrhea and chlamydia. Fred Evans, coordinator of community health for the Fremont clinic, says it is important to engage teenage boys in dialogues about birth control and STDs because they rarely initiate such discussions on their own. "Unless they're burning, leaking or dripping [they don't see a doctor]," says Evans. "It's a macho image. It's 'I can handle it myself.'" As for Grady, he believes he has reached many boys and has convinced them of the importance of using condoms.

Quoted in Gail Rosenblum, "What About the Guys?," *Minneapolis Star Tribune*, May 1, 2008. www.startribune.com.

describes her ideal sex education class: "[It should include] a demonstration on how to use a condom; learning about heterosexual and homosexual relationships; different types of birth control; and the . . . different types of sex. . . . You would learn about romantic relationships and about the different things you can do to prevent actual intercourse but still be romantic."[87]

Some schools have taken a dim view when students promote condom use. In 2001 Lissette Stanley, the senior class president of Blake High School in Hillsborough County, Florida, inserted condoms into giveaway bags distributed to students at her school's prom. The school board had established a firm policy against distributing condoms to students. When school administrators learned of Stanley's action, they stripped the student of her presidency and denied her the opportunity to make a graduation speech. "We don't want to encourage students to be sexually active by distributing condoms,"[88] said Mark Hart, the spokesman for the Hillsborough County School District. Stanley responded that she inserted the condoms in the giveaway bags with good intentions. "I just thought I should put that in there because I thought the kids need protection,"[89] she said.

"We don't want to encourage students to be sexually active by distributing condoms."[88]

— Mark Hart, spokesman for the Hillsborough County School District in Florida.

Students Still Take Chances

The fact that as many as 30 percent of American high schools are willing to provide contraceptives to students indicates that many educators have concluded that no matter how much they preach a message of abstinence, some students are still going to have sex. These educators realize that although abstinence may be the right message, the consequences of ignoring teen sex are too grave to ignore. School administrators in Gloucester, Massachusetts, learned about those consequences when eighteen girls, none older than sixteen, got pregnant in the course of a single year. In Portland, Maine, school administrators took the difficult and controversial step of making condoms available in middle schools due to a rash of teen pregnancies among even younger students.

Meanwhile, many schools that do not provide contraceptives still help students obtain them; they refer girls to women's health

Students watch as an instructor demonstrates the use of a condom. Some school districts support programs that include frank discussions of sex and birth control while others believe such programs encourage sexual activity.

clinics and boys to outreach programs that provide condoms. Because of a change in attitude by retailers since the 1980s—due to the recognition that condoms are an effective means of preventing STDs—adolescents find that buying prophylactics in the neighborhood pharmacy is no longer the terrifying experience it was years ago.

As contraception has become widely accessible, some students are nevertheless still willing to abstain from sex, but others feel they need to ask the school nurse to provide condoms or birth control pills. Some students know their friends are taking chances. That is why they have joined Sex, Etc., Planned Parenthood teen councils, and similar groups, hoping that they can exert more influence on their friends than their sex education teachers are able to provide.

Facts

- In twenty-six states and Washington, DC, students are able to obtain contraceptives in their schools without their parents' approval, the *Christian Science Monitor* reported in 2010. In all other states, students must have the permission of their parents to obtain contraceptives.

- The Provincetown School District in Massachusetts commenced a program in 2010 to distribute condoms to students, starting in the fifth grade. The students do not need their parents' permission to obtain the condoms.

- A 2010 poll conducted by the online publishing service Helium.com found that 61 percent of its twenty-one hundred respondents supported the distribution of condoms in public schools.

- New York City runs an annual contest to design the wrappers for the condoms the city distributes to high school students and others. In 2010, the first year of the contest, the competition drew entries from nearly six hundred artists. The winner was picked through on-line voting in which more than fifteen thousand ballots were cast.

- A 2011 study by Baystate Children's Hospital in Massachusetts found that the rates of gonorrhea and chlamydia among male high school students in Holyoke, Massachusetts, were 47 percent lower than those recorded in the nearby city of Springfield. Schools in Holyoke distribute condoms to students, but schools in Springfield do not.

How Can Sex Education Programs Be Improved?

When Jewels Morris-Davis reached the age of sixteen, she was proud of an important accomplishment: she had avoided parenthood as a teenager and was certain that she would continue to make smart decisions about sex. "I am the first person in my family to reach 16 without getting pregnant—or getting somebody pregnant,"[90] she says.

At times it appeared Morris-Davis was on track to suffer the same fate as others in her family. The daughter of a drug-addicted mother, Morris-Davis was being raised by her grandmother. When her grandmother died of cancer, Morris-Davis found herself in foster care. She turned to sex in search of the loving relationship she found missing at home.

Morris-Davis believes she was saved from teenage pregnancy or an STD by Impact, a teen pregnancy prevention program adopted by her high school in Anderson County, South Carolina. Alarmed by a high teen pregnancy rate, administrators at Crescent High School contracted with the Anderson Oconee Council on

Teen Pregnancy Prevention to provide the Impact program, which the council regards as a comprehensive sex education course. Impact stresses both abstinence and safe sex, but it also has a third component: young people learn values as well as decision-making skills that help them make the right choices when it comes to sex.

A New Attitude

The fact that Morris-Davis's school turned to Impact illustrates that many educators are rethinking their sex education programs and concluding that they must cover more than information about abstinence, safe sex, unwanted pregnancies, and STDs. This new attitude may be largely driven by the students themselves, who have been telling experts for years that they find their sex education classes inadequate. "Our young people are clamoring for sex education," says the actress and social activist Jane Fonda. "Time and time again, we hear from high school students saying the sex education they receive is inadequate, it comes too late, and it does not teach them the skills they need to act responsibly."[91]

In 2011 the University of North Florida's Brooks College of Health in Jacksonville, Florida, conducted a forum with area high school students to find out what they thought of their sex education classes. The researchers were astonished at the responses they heard from the students: the sex education teachers seemed to be in a rush to finish the classes; the classes focused mostly on puberty, hygiene, and abstinence; and they provided little information about STDs and condom use. The students said they found it difficult to obtain contraceptives in the Jacksonville area, and even those students who could obtain condoms said they were not convinced they were effective.

James Beattie, a YMCA youth counselor who sat in on the forum, says he was not surprised by the answers. "They often come to me with these sort of questions," he says. "They want to know what is good about sex and what is bad about sex; the emotional stuff that comes along with it. They're curious about the whole thing."[92]

"Time and time again, we hear from high school students saying the sex education they receive is inadequate, it comes too late, and it does not teach them the skills they need to act responsibly."[91]

— Actress and social activist Jane Fonda.

Combating Gender Stereotypes

One answer that emerged from the Brooks College forum was the contention by the boys that birth control is primarily the girl's responsibility. To sex education experts, this response indicates that the male students lack the values that should be telling them that contraception is the responsibility of both partners. "Gender stereotypes—for example, it's the girl's responsibility to bring up birth control—are still very strong," says Monica Rodriguez, president of the Sexuality Information and Education Council of the United States (SIECUS). "Look at the images. In women's magazines, you don't see guys in the ads for the birth control patch or the pill. And you don't see condoms in men's magazines very often."[93]

Programs like Impact are trying to change those attitudes. The program not only provides information about sex, but it also tries to change young people's feelings about taking responsibility and looking ahead toward the consequences of unprotected sex.

Impact is different from the programs found in other schools. Impact teacher Kristen Jordan—an employee with the Anderson Oconee Council—teaches sex education from the elementary grades through high school. Her first job is to show the younger students that sex is a topic that can be discussed openly and that they should not keep their doubts and fears about the subject to themselves. In the sixth grade, for example, students can be heard shouting the words "Penis! Penis! Penis!" and "Vagina! Vagina! Vagina!" from the classroom. Says Jordan, "Until they [learn to] use real names for their body parts without giggling, you can't talk to them about anything serious."[94]

"Gender stereotypes—for example, it's the girl's responsibility to bring up birth control—are still very strong."[93]

— Monica Rodriguez, president of the Sexuality Information and Education Council of the United States.

Enhancing Self-Esteem

In middle school and high school, Jordan's classes address contraception, abstinence, STDs, and other topics found in most other sex education courses, but the classes are also designed to enhance the self-esteem of the students. One method is a role-playing game in which the students take turns pressuring part-

ners for sex and learning how to resist the pressure.

One class is devoted to what Impact regards as high-risk students—young people whose siblings are already teen parents. In the class for the high-risk students, Jordan's students will see posters on the walls proclaiming, "Not Me, Not Now" and "Self-Respect: The Ultimate Contraceptive."

In addition to the classroom work, the Anderson Oconee Council has organized community service projects—such as volunteering at homeless shelters—to help young people learn values and team-building skills. Moreover, the program includes fun activities, such as bowling parties, and activities for students over the summer months designed to ensure that messages taught during the school year stay with the students during their vacations.

Jordan has been able to connect with the students. They regard her as a reliable source of sexuality information who can provide serious answers to their questions. (In one case, a student wanted to know whether drinking Mountain Dew would lower his sperm count. No, she told him, it would not.)

Students opposed to abstinence-only education in Britain publicly express their views. Many, though not all, students in the United States also say they want more information about sex and sexuality in their sex education classes.

Impact Shows Results

Impact seems to be working. Prior to the first year of the program in 2004, about twenty Anderson County students a year were getting pregnant. Five years later, teen pregnancies in Anderson County dropped to one or two a year. Douglas Kirby, an authority on sex education, believes the Impact program offers an effective method of convincing young people to delay sex or at least to practice safe sex. "The older programs were less likely to deliver a clear message about behavior," Kirby says. "It was, 'Here are the facts, here are the pros and cons. You decide what's right for you.' [Impact has] a very clear message that not having sex is the safest choice. They put emphasis on skill-building and role-playing, they teach how to use condoms, and they encourage young people not to have sex."[95]

Morris-Davis has certainly absorbed the message. She has avoided teen pregnancy, stayed in school, and has joined the track team and cheerleading squad. "I don't need anyone to tell me I'm beautiful," she says. "I know I'm beautiful. I'm going to be the first one in my family to graduate from high school. I'm going to college. And then I'll get a job. And then I want to be married . . . with no kids."[96]

> "I'm going to be the first one in my family to graduate from high school. I'm going to college. And then I'll get a job. And then I want to be married . . . with no kids."[96]
>
> — Jewels Morris-Davis, a student at Crescent High School in South Carolina.

An Above-the-Waist Approach

Impact is the type of program that might find wider acceptance in American schools due to a change in how the federal government funds sex education. When the Obama administration reduced federal funding for abstinence-only education, it sought to encourage school districts to adopt programs like Impact. Over a five-year period beginning in 2010, the administration was making $375 million available to states, local school districts, and non-profit organizations that demonstrated innovative ways to prevent teen pregnancies and the spread of STDs.

One organization that has grown in popularity among educators is the Carrera Adolescent Pregnancy Prevention Program, which focuses on low-income young people. In addition to sex

Does Abstinence-Only Sex Education Have a Future?

Following the Obama administration's decision to scale back funding for abstinence-only sex education, many states dropped out of the plan to pursue programs that would qualify for the $375 million the administration budgeted for results-oriented programs. However, in a compromise with conservative lawmakers, the administration agreed to provide $50 million over five years to continue funding abstinence-only programs.

According to a 2011 University of Tennessee study, twenty-one states have elected to continue with abstinence-only education but now find themselves having to share a mere $10 million a year in federal funding to help finance sex education in their schools. As the study explains, "The states that supported abstinence-only are currently scrambling to secure private funding to keep those programs afloat."

One school district that still believes in abstinence-only education is the West Independent School District in McLennan County, Texas. Since 2006 a nonprofit group, the McLennan County Collaborative Abstinence Program (MCCAP), had been receiving $1 million a year in state and federal grants for the abstinence-only programs it conducts in West Independent schools. In 2009 those funds all but disappeared. "It was a definite shock to go from everything we had down to the bare minimum," says Tracy Cousins, executive director of MCCAP. To make up the shortfall, MCCAP has turned to private donors.

Jennifer S. Hendricks, "Teaching Values, Teaching Stereotypes: Sex Ed and Indoctrination in Public Schools," Tennessee Research and Creative Exchange, 2011. http://trace.tennessee.edu.

Quoted in Sarah Kliff, "The Future of Abstinence," Daily Beast, October 26, 2009. www.thedaily beast.com.

education, the Carrera program also provides classes for students in music, art, and science and sponsors field trips, homework tutoring, mental health counseling, and free medical and dental care. The program helps students find summer jobs, open bank accounts, and learn how to balance their checkbooks.

According to Michael A. Carrera, the City University of New York professor who designed the program, and Richard Buery, president of the New York–based Children's Aid Society,

> This model is proven to help young girls and boys avoid becoming parents during the second decade of their lives. The "above the waist," long-term approach ensures effectiveness by combining academic enrichment, mental health services, family life and sexuality education, understanding the world of work, sports, self-expression, and comprehensive no cost medical and dental care during the school day. . . .
>
> It is this dosage and duration that make an essential difference. Adults do not reduce teen pregnancy and births; young people do. They achieve this through educational repetitions centered on the benefits of abstinence, the importance of acquiring sexual and reproductive health knowledge, the conscientious use of contraceptives, the essential importance of acquiring primary health care, and the life-long benefits of educational achievement and developing aspirations for a career or profession.[97]

The Long-Term Impact

By 2012 numerous school districts had adopted the Carrera program. In Wilmington, Delaware, the city school system obtained a $2.9 million federal grant in 2010 to launch the program. Wilmington officials provided a neighborhood center where participants attend the Carerra program six days a week over the course of a year. Wilmington officials elected to try the Carerra program in response to an epidemic of teen pregnancies. According to 2007 statistics—the latest available—221 mothers aged nineteen and younger gave birth in the city that year. Moreover, about 11 percent of those mothers were students in the ninth grade or below. "If that isn't a disaster, I don't know what is,"[98] says Wilmington mayor James M. Baker.

Di'Andra Woody, a twelve-year-old seventh-grade student, signed up for Wilmington's Carerra program. "It will help me know about the dangers out there in the world and how having sex at an early age will ruin my life," she says. "If I'm planning on going to college and then getting a job, it would ruin my chances of doing that early, because I will have to stay home and take care of the baby."[99]

The Carerra sex education model was also adopted by a nonprofit group, the Children's Home Society of West Virginia, which has employed it in three cities: Parkersburg, Martinsburg, and Clarksburg. The program reaches about sixty students a year. Unlike the yearlong Carerra programs in other cities, though, the West Virginia project is designed to be attended by the students over a period of five years. The program starts with students in the sixth grade. "The basic premise is, the children that are at-risk or low income are often in the demographic to become teen parents,"

Community service projects, such as food drives, that help teens learn values and team-building skills are considered one way to redirect at-risk teens toward healthy activities. Such programs urge young people to delay sex or at least to practice safe sex.

says Steve Tuck, site director for the program in Parkersburg. "In our model, it's based on the idea that you are going to be having this impact over a longer period of time."[100]

When Should Sex Education Begin?

Although programs like Impact and Carrera may be effective, in many places parents are still uncomfortable with the notion of introducing young children—such as the sixth-grade students in West Virginia—to sex education. Organizations like SIECUS may encourage sex education in the earliest stages of elementary school, but the question of when children are old enough to absorb those lessons often remains in doubt.

In Helena, Montana, school administrators proposed a sex education curriculum in 2010 designed to include more than just lessons on abstinence, contraception, and STDs. As with the Impact and Carrera programs, the Helena program also features components of community involvement, nutrition, and physical education—all designed to introduce students to values and self-esteem building.

However, the Helena program was structured to begin in kindergarten, where the district's youngest students would learn the names of sexual organs. In the first grade, students would be introduced to the concept that two people of the same gender can love each other. By the fifth grade, students would learn about intercourse—including vaginal, oral, and anal. In defense of the program, school officials pointed out that under the new curriculum, education about sex would be incorporated into other topics. For the youngest students, the lessons would also include education about other body parts as well as the five senses and how they are useful in keeping the body healthy. The youngest students would also be taught about safe and unsafe hygiene.

More Emphasis on Abstinence

When the students reached the fourth grade, the Helena curriculum called for students to learn about how their bodies change during puberty—both physically and emotionally. At this level, they were also to be given their first lessons about STDs.

In the fifth grade, the curriculum was planned to include lessons about the male and female reproductive systems. For many of these discussions, students would be separated into groups according to gender. In class, they would be given opportunities to ask anonymous questions. If teachers believed that some students were having trouble understanding the concepts covered in class, they would be referred to individual counselors. "It's good, factual information,"[101] insists Ruth Uecker, superintendent of elementary education for the Helena schools.

Standardized Testing for Sex Education

Students take standardized tests to gauge their proficiencies in mathematics, reading comprehension, and other core subjects. Soon standardized testing for sex education may become common as well.

In 2012 school officials in Washington, DC, instituted a citywide standardized test to find out how much students know about contraception, STDs, and similar topics. School officials stressed that the tests are provided to help administrators determine whether sex education programs in city schools are effective. Mark Jones, a member of the Washington, DC, school board and a parent of two children in city schools, says, "I don't think our children understand enough on STDs and high-risk behavior. . . . We need to know more." The tests are administered to students in the fifth, eighth, and tenth grades.

In announcing plans for the test, school officials noted that a 2009 study found that nearly half of the city's gonorrhea and chlamydia cases are contracted by people between the ages of fifteen and nineteen and that some of the city's AIDS patients are as young as twelve.

Quoted in Bill Turque, "D.C. Schools Prepare for Nation's First Sex-Education Standardized Testing," *Washington Post*, September 14, 2011. www.washingtonpost.com.

Still, many parents found Helena's approach to sex education too frank for the younger elementary school students. "Why do they have to learn such a list of reproductive body parts?" asks Cindy Bacon, the mother of a Helena kindergarten student. "I have no problem with basic body parts being taught, but . . . my 5-year-old girl has no need to understand the scrotum or testicles at this point."[102]

School officials countered that a change in how Helena schools teach sex education was in order, citing studies that showed some 50 percent of the city's high school students are sexually active. However, after a public hearing Helena officials agreed to alter the new program, dropping much of the content that was aimed at the very youngest students. Helena educators also agreed to put more of an emphasis on abstinence for the fifth-grade students, but other than that change, the course material for those students remained intact.

Parents Can Do More

Perhaps parents in Helena and elsewhere would not be as hostile to sex education in the earliest grades if they paid more attention to the matter at home. According to a 2009 study by Children's Hospital in Boston, a large proportion of parents do not even begin to talk about sex with their sons and daughters until after their children have already become sexually active. In fact, the study shows that 40 percent of teenage girls have never talked about birth control with their parents, and 42 percent of girls have never talked with their parents about how to refuse sex. In addition, the researchers found that 70 percent of teenage boys have never discussed using a condom with their parents.

Karen Soren, director of adolescent medicine at New York Presbyterian Hospital, says many parents fear the topic and even many of those who do talk about sex with their sons and daughters tend to be evasive when discussing the subject. Knowing they should discuss sex with their preadolescent and adolescent children, Soren says, many parents attempt to broach the topic in vague terms, then hope their teenagers get the message. "Parents sometimes say things more vaguely because they are uncomfortable and they think they've addressed something, but the kids don't hear the topic at all,"[103] she says.

The National Campaign to Prevent Teen and Unplanned Pregnancy believes parental guidance—starting with talking about sex—can be one of the most effective means to reduce teen pregnancies and the spread of STDs. And surveys show that young people do want to talk about these matters with their parents. A 2011 Canadian study by the University of Montreal found that nearly half of the students polled say they look to their parents for guidance on sex. "Parents probably are shy to discuss sexuality and perhaps enter into that domain because they think they are not in the game—which is not true," says study coauthor Jean-Yves Frappier. "Yes, [teens] want to become independent, but what we forget is that they have been living with their parents for years and they are probably still very important. We forget Britney Spears and Brad Pitt are only pictures. Parents are the real substance."[104]

"Parents sometimes [talk about sex] more vaguely because they are uncomfortable and they think they've addressed something, but the kids don't hear the topic at all."[103]

— Karen Soren, director of adolescent medicine at New York Presbyterian Hospital.

Sex Education Moves Ahead

As the case in Helena illustrates, nearly a century after sex education was first introduced into American schools, it continues to be a controversial topic with little agreement on how best to teach it. Over the years two extreme views have emerged: On the one hand, many people continue to hold to the notion that abstinence is the only effective method for young people to avoid unwanted pregnancies and STDs. On the other side, many people believe that while abstinence should be stressed, young people should be taught about contraceptives and how to use them.

Clearly, no system has proven to be perfect. Over the past century educators have tried to scare young people into remaining abstinent by telling them of the horrors of STDs—particularly AIDS, which can be fatal. For the young draftees on their way to war, sex educators tried to deliver a message of patriotism—telling them that contracting an STD would hurt the war effort as much as their being felled by the enemy. Some educators have focused on the burden teenage parents face as they tend to their infants. To drive the point home, some of these classes make students care for mechanical dolls that start crying in the early hours of the morning, demanding to be fed.

And yet teenage girls continue to get pregnant, and adolescents of both genders continue to contract STDs. As American sex education moves ahead, and educators focus more on teaching about values and responsibility, many hope that this formula will help cut down on the teen pregnancy and STD rates and, perhaps, make teenagers into better people overall.

Facts

- The Carrera Adolescent Pregnancy Prevention Program was first adopted by schools in 2007. In 2010 a review of the program's effectiveness found that teenage girls who participated had a pregnancy rate 47 percent lower than girls who did not take the course.

- The Guttmacher Institute reported in 2012 that 79 percent of teenage girls and 70 percent of teenage boys have talked to their parents about sex. Topics discussed among parents and their adolescent children included how to say no to sex, how to use contraception, and STDs.

- In 2012 the National Conference of State Legislatures reported that eighteen states require medical accuracy in sex ed classes, meaning the information must be verified by legitimate medical sources.

- A 2012 study by New York University and the Planned Parenthood Federation of America found that 43 percent of parents are "very comfortable" talking about sex with their children, with the remainder feeling either "somewhat comfortable" or "uncomfortable" while having discussions about sex with their children.

Source Notes

Introduction: Does Sex Education in American Schools Need to Be Fixed?

1. Quoted in Chantalle Carles, "Contraceptives in Middle Schools," Alachuapost.com, November 20, 2007. http://alachuapost.com.

2. Quoted in Healthy Teens Campaign, "Alachua," 2010. http://healthy teensflorida.org.

3. Quoted in Jackie Alexander, "More Emphasis Needed on Preventing Teen Pregnancies, Officials Say," *Gainesville (FL) Sun*, March 13, 2012. www .gainesville.com.

4. Quoted in Alexander, "More Emphasis Needed on Preventing Teen Pregnancies, Officials Say."

5. Quoted in Lynn Moore, "Muskegon School Board Members Defend New Sex Ed Curriculum," *Muskegon (MI) Chronicle*, March 13, 2012. www.mlive.com.

6. Susie Wilson, "It's All About Prevention: The Purpose of Sex Education," September 24, 2009. www.newjerseynewsroom.com.

7. Joycelyn M. Elders, foreword to *Harmful to Minors: The Perils of Protecting Children from Sex,* by Judith Levine. Minneapolis: University of Minnesota Press, 2002, p. ix.

Chapter One: What Are the Origins of the Sex Education Controversy?

8. Thomas Washington Shannon, *Guide to Sex: Vital Facts of Life for All Ages.* Marietta, OH: S.A. Mullikin, 1913, p. 201.

9. Julian B. Carter, "Birds, Bees, and Venereal Disease: Toward an Intellectual History of Sex Education," *Journal of the History of Sexuality*, April 2001, p. 225.

10. Ira Solomon Wile, *Sex Education*. New York: Duffield, 1912, p. 38.

11. Quoted in Elizabeth Gettleman and Mark Murrmann, "Enemy in Your Pants: The Military's Decades-Long War Against STDs," *Mother Jones*, May 2010. http://motherjones.com.

12. Quoted in Kristin Luker, *When Sex Goes to School: Warring Views on Sex—and Sex Education—Since the Sixties*. New York: W.W. Norton, 2006, p. 54.

13. Charles E. Brown, "The Hippies of Haight Hashberry," *Ebony*, August 1967, p. 118.

14. Quoted in John Kobler, "Sex Invades the Schoolhouse," *Saturday Evening Post*, June 29, 1968, p. 24.

15. Quoted in *Washington Post*, "Appeal for Funds in Falwell's Campaign on Sex Education Has 'Filthy Material,'" November 21, 1980, p. F10.

16. Quoted in Cliff Yudell, "Pastor, Evangelist, Crusader," *Saturday Evening Post*, May/June 1981, p. 128.

17. Quoted in Sandra G. Boodman, "Surgeon General, at Falwell's College, Urges AIDS Prevention," *New York Times*, January 20, 1987, p. B1.

18. Quoted in Robert Preidt, "Study Links Viewing Adult-Themed TV to Earlier Sex in Teens," *USA Today*, May 7, 2009. www.usatoday.com.

19. Quoted in MSNBC, "Dirty Song Lyrics Can Prompt Early Teen Sex," August 7, 2006. www.msnbc.msn.com.

20. Quoted in John Keilman, "Teens and Online Porn: Is It as 'Damaging' as Santorum Says?," *Chicago Tribune*, March 25, 2012. http://articles.chicagotribune.com.

21. Michael Castleman, "How Does Internet Porn Affect Teens—Really?," *Psychology Today*, May 17, 2011. www.psychologytoday.com/blog/all-about-sex/201105/how-does-internet-porn-affect-teens-really.

22. Quoted in Hannah Deely, "We Are Not Going to Screw This Up," *Us Weekly*, March 19, 2012, p. 49.

Chapter Two: Should Schools Focus on Abstinence or Safe Sex?

23. Quoted in Vania Cao, "Teen Parents Struggle to Find a Life Between Being a Child and Having One," *Centre Daily Times* (State College, PA), June 6, 2002.

24. Quoted in Cao, "Teen Parents Struggle to Find a Life Between Being a Child and Having One."

25. Quoted in Cao, "Teen Parents Struggle to Find a Life Between Being a Child and Having One."

26. Valerie Huber, "Best Message Is Abstinence," *USA Today*, September 3, 2008, p. 14A.

27. Quoted in Katy Vine, "Faith, Hope, and Chastity," *Texas Monthly*, May 2008, p. 134.

28. Quoted in Vine, "Faith, Hope, and Chastity," p. 134.

29. Paul Weyrich, "Abstinence Education Works," Renew America, February 15, 2005, www.renewamerica.com.

30. Quoted in Jessica Crawford, "Course Teaches Abstinence: Why It's an Important Choice for Students," *Liberal (Kansas) Southwest Daily Times*, February 2006. www.choosingthebest.org.

31. Quoted in Stephanie Booth, "Why Sex Ed Sucks," *Teen People*, October 2001, p. 124.

32. Quoted in Sharon Cromwell, "'Baby' Helps Teens Think It Over!," Education World, 2010. www.educationworld.com.

33. Quoted in *Curriculum Review*, "Belly Up to the Empathy Belly?," September 2001, p. 11.

34. Quoted in *Curriculum Review*, "Belly Up to the Empathy Belly?," p. 11.

35. Quoted in Gracie Bonds Staples, "Learning to Say N-O to S-E-X: With Abstinence Pledge Becoming Popular, Schools Consider Adding It to Curriculum," *Atlanta Journal-Constitution*, January 15, 2011, p. D1.

36. Retreat Evangelization and Prayer, "Athlete's Choice for Chastity," 2012. www.reapteam.org.

37. Quoted in Katy Kelly, "Just Don't Do It," *US News & World Report*, October 17, 2005, p. 44.

38. Quoted in Kelly, "Just Don't Do It," p. 44.

39. Quoted in Laurie Abraham, "Teaching Good Sex," *New York Times Magazine*, November 20, 2011, p. 36.

40. Quoted in Abraham, "Teaching Good Sex," p. 36.

41. Quoted in Abraham, "Teaching Good Sex," p. 36.

42. Quoted in Abraham, "Teaching Good Sex," p. 36.

43. Quoted in Molly Masland, "Carnal Knowledge: The Sex Ed Debate," MSNBC, September 17, 2010. www.msnbc.msn.com.

44. Quoted in Landon Hall, "Abstinence Programs, Teen Pregnancy Linked?," *Orange County Register*, January 27, 2010.

45. Brady E. Hamilton and Stephanie J. Ventura, "Birth Rates for U.S. Teenagers Reach Historic Lows for All Age and Ethnic Groups," Centers for Disease Control and Prevention, April 2012. www.cdc.gov.

46. Quoted in Kelly, "Just Don't Do It," p. 44.

47. Quoted in Kelly, "Just Don't Do It," p. 44.

48. Quoted in *District Administration*, "Abstinence, Contraception Frame Sex Education," January 2011, p. 73.

Chapter Three: Should Schools Teach About Homosexuality?

49. Robert Skutch, *Who's in a Family?* Berkeley, CA: Tricycle, 1995, pp. 2, 21.

50. Quoted in Jake Tapper, "Culture War Hits Kindergarten," ABC News, October 19, 2005. http://abcnews.go.com.

51. Quoted in Tapper, "Culture War Hits Kindergarten."

52. Quoted in Sarah Miller Llana, "New Flash Point in Sex Ed: Gay Issues," *Christian Science Monitor*, Februrary 15, 2006, p. 2.

53. Quoted in Diane Jean Schemo, "Lessons on Homosexuality Move into Classroom," *New York Times*, August 15, 2007. www.nytimes.com.

54. Quoted in Kelly, "Just Don't Do It," p. 44.

55. Quoted in Schemo, "Lessons on Homosexuality Move into Classroom."

56. Quoted in Schemo, "Lessons on Homosexuality Move into Classroom."

57. Quoted in Billy Hallowell, "New Sex Ed Standards Call for Homosexuality to Be Explained to 5th-Graders," *Blaze*, January 9, 2012. www.theblaze.com.

58. Quoted in Hallowell, "New Sex Ed Standards Call for Homosexuality to Be Explained to 5th-Graders."

59. Quoted in Connie Schultz, "Parma High Schools Teens Make a Request for Real Sex Education," *Cleveland Plain Dealer*, February 24, 2010. www.cleveland.com.

60. Quoted in Susan Ketchum, "Parma Graduate Still Seeking More Comprehensive Sex Education Program in School," *Cleveland News Sun*, June 9, 2011. http://blog.cleveland.com.

61. Quoted in Ketchum, "Parma Graduate Still Seeking More Comprehensive Sex Education Program in School."

62. Quoted in Lisa Schencker, "Legislature Passes Bill to Let Schools Drop Sex Education," *Salt Lake Tribune*, March 6, 2012. www.sltrib.com.

63. Quoted in Schencker, "Legislature Passes Bill to Let Schools Drop Sex Education."

64. Quoted in Chas Sisk, "Lawmakers Back Away from Don't Say Gay Bill," *Nashville Tennessean*, March 13, 2012. www.tennessean.com.

65. Quoted in Stacy Teicher Khadaroo, "Death of California Youth Puts Focus on Rise in Antigay Bullying," *Christian Science Monitor*, September 29, 2010, p. 1.

66. Gay, Lesbian & Straight Education Network, "2009 National School Climate Survey: Nearly 9 out of 10 Students Experience Harassment in School," September 14, 2010. www.glsen.org.

67. Quoted in Kelly Smith, "Anoka-Hennepin Sued over Bullying," *Minneapolis (MN) Star-Tribune*, July 22, 2011. www.startribune.com.

68. Quoted in Erik Eckholm, "Eight Suicides in Two Years in District," *New York Times*, September 13, 2011, p. A4.

69. Quoted in Stephanie Mencimer, "The Teen Suicide Epidemic in Michele Bachmann's District," *Mother Jones*, July 25, 2011. http://motherjones.com.

Chapter Four: Should Schools Do More than Teach About Sex?

70. Quoted in Gretchen Voss, "Inside the Gloucester Pregnancy Pact," *Marie Claire*, October 2008. www.marieclaire.com.

71. Sexuality Information and Education Council of the United States, "Guidelines for Comprehensive Sexuality Education: Kindergarten Through 12th Grade," 2004, p. 13. www2.gsu.edu.

72. Quoted in Katie Zezima, "Spike in School's Pregnancies Leads to Report That Some Resulted from Girls' Pact," *New York Times*, June 20, 2008, p. A15.

73. Quoted in Patrick Anderson, "School to Dispense Birth Control," *Gloucester Times*, October 9, 2008. www.gloucestertimes.com.

74. Quoted in Bonnie Rochman, "Half of Teen Moms Don't Use Birth Control —Why That's No Surprise," *Time*, January 20, 2012. http://healthland. time.com.

75. Quoted in *New York Amsterdam News*, "Study Shows Most Drug Stores Discourage the Sale of Condoms," October 31, 1992, p. 15.

76. Quoted in Jacqueline Henry, "Myths Cloud Teenagers' Knowledge of Sexuality," *New York Times*, January 19, 1997, p. LI-1.

77. Quoted in E.R. Shipp, "Sex and School Clinic: City at Odds," *New York Times*, September 22, 1985, p. 26.

78. Quoted in Joseph Berger, "What Students Think About Condom Plan," *New York Times*, September 28, 1990, p. B1.

79. Quoted in Cheryl Wetzstein, "AMA Policy Backs Giving Out Condoms; GOP Doctor Calls Line Irresponsible," *Washington Times*, December 16, 1999, p. 4.

80. Quoted in Katie Zezima, "Not All Are Pleased at Plan to Offer Birth Control at Maine Middle School," *New York Times*, October 21, 2007. www.nytimes.com.

81. Quoted in Zezima, "Not All Are Pleased at Plan to Offer Birth Control at Maine Middle School."

82. Quoted in Zezima, "Not All Are Pleased at Plan to Offer Birth Control at Maine Middle School."

83. Quoted in Cao, "Teen Parents Struggle to Find a Life Between Being a Child and Having One."

84. Quoted in Whitney Malkin, "Students Stand Up for Sex Education," *Eugene (OR) Register-Guard*, October 15, 2007, p. C17.

85. Quoted in Gail Rosenblum, "What About the Guys?," *Minneapolis Star Tribune*, May 1, 2008. www.startribune.com.

86. Quoted in Melissa Daly, "Baby Blues," *Human Sexuality*, March 2006, p. 1.

87. Quoted in Kelly, "Just Don't Do It," p. 44.

88. Quoted in ABC News, "Class President Sacked for Prom Condom Giveaway," May 29, 2001. http://abcnews.go.com.

89. Quoted in ABC News, "Class President Sacked for Prom Condom Giveaway."

90. Quoted in Amy Sullivan Anderson, "How to Bring an End to the War over Sex Ed," *Time*, March 19, 2009. www.time.com.

91. Jane Fonda, "Abstinence-Only-Until-Marriage Programs Have Not Reduced Teen Pregnancy," Huffington Post, April 17, 2009. www.huffing tonpost.com.

92. Quoted in Joel Addington, "Teens to Researchers: Sex Ed Inadequate," *Baker County (FL) Press*, March 3, 2011. www.bakercountypress.com.

93. Quoted in Karen Baar, "What Is Intimacy?," *Human Sexuality*, October 2005, p. 1.

94. Quoted in Anderson, "How to Bring an End to the War over Sex Ed."

95. Quoted in Anderson, "How to Bring an End to the War over Sex Ed."

96. Quoted in Anderson, "How to Bring an End to the War over Sex Ed."

97. Richard Buery and Michael A. Carrera, "Revamping Sex Education: A New Approach to the Birds and the Bees," Huffington Post, October 6, 2011. www.huffingtonpost.com.

98. Quoted in Adam Taylor, "City Teen Pregnancy Targeted," *Wilmington News Journal*, October 22, 2010.

99. Quoted in Taylor, "City Teen Pregnancy Targeted."

100. Quoted in Veronica Nett, "Grants Offer New Approach to Teen Pregnancy," *Charleston Gazette*, October 21, 2010, p. A3.

101. Quoted in Kristen Cates, "No Local Drama Over Sex Ed Curriculum," *Great Falls (MT) Tribune*, August 1, 2010, p. M1.

102. Quoted in Alana Listoe, "Sex Education Causes Stir in Helena Public Schools," *Helena (MT) Independent Record*, June 9, 2010. http://helenair. com.

103. Quoted in Alice Park, "Parents' Sex Talk with Kids: Too Little, Too Late," *Time*, December 7, 2009. www.time.com.

104. Quoted in Laura Baziuk, "Teens Look to Parents as Sex Role Models More than Friends, Study Says," *Montreal (CQ) Gazette*, June 15, 2011. www.montrealgazette.com.

Related Organizations and Websites

Abstinence and Marriage Education Partnership

411 Business Center Dr., Suite 103
Mount Prospect, IL 60056
phone: (224) 735-3622
fax: (224) 735-3624
website: www.ampartnership.org

This group designs abstinence-only curricula for schools and also maintains a speakers' bureau of abstinence-only advocates who address students and other groups. By following the "Curriculum" link on the organization's website, visitors can find publications and classroom materials stressing the partnership's abstinence-only message.

Advocates for Youth

2000 M St. NW, Suite 750
Washington, DC 20036
phone: (202) 419-3420
fax: (202) 419-1448
website: www.advocatesforyouth.org

Advocates for Youth works to enhance sex education in American schools. Students can find many resources about adolescent sexuality on the organization's website. By accessing the "Topics & Issues" link, visitors can find statistics and other facts about contraceptive use, abstinence-only education, abortion, and homosexuality.

Centers for Disease Control and Prevention (CDC)

4770 Buford Hwy.
Atlanta, GA 30341-3717
phone: (800) 232-4636
website: www.cdc.gov

The federal government's primary public health agency, the CDC examines many issues relating to adolescent sexuality, including teenage pregnancy and the spread of STDs. Visitors to the CDC's website can access the reports *STDs in Adolescents and Young Adults* and *About Teen Pregnancy*.

Gay, Lesbian & Straight Education Network (GLSEN)

90 Broad St., 2nd Floor
New York, NY 10004
phone: (212) 727-0135
fax: (212) 727-0254
email: glsen@glsen.org
website: www.glsen.org

The GLSEN is dedicated to ensuring that gay students are treated equally in schools. Visitors to the GLSEN website can find many reports chronicling harassment and bullying against gay students in American schools as well as studies on how abstinence-only sex education does not adequately address the needs of gay students.

Guttmacher Institute

125 Maiden Ln., 7th Floor
New York, NY 10038
phone: (800) 355-0244
fax: (212) 248-1951
website: www.guttmacher.org

The institute studies sexuality trends in America, including trends involving young people. By following the "Adolescents" link on the institute's website, students can access many studies, including the 2012 reports *Facts on American Teens' Sexual and Reproductive Health* and *Facts on American Teens' Sources of Information About Sex*.

National Abstinence Education Association (NAEA)

1701 Pennsylvania Ave. NW, Suite 300
Washington, DC 20006
phone: (202) 248-5420
fax: (866) 935-4850
email: info@theNAEA.org
website: www.abstinenceassociation.org

The NAEA lobbies Congress and state legislatures to maintain funding for abstinence-only education programs. By accessing the "Advocacy" link on the organization's website, students can find commentaries by NAEA leaders on sex education policies, including the Obama administration's decision to scale back funding for abstinence-only programs.

National Campaign to Prevent Teen and Unplanned Pregnancy

1776 Massachusetts Ave. NW, Suite 200
Washington, DC 20036
phone: (202) 478-8500
fax: (202) 478-8588
website: www.thenationalcampaign.org

This organization collects data on teenage pregnancies and provides grants to groups that develop programs aimed at helping young people avoid becoming parents. Students can find many resources on the organization's website, including national and state-by-state teen pregnancy statistics.

Parents and Friends of Ex-Gays and Gays (PFOX)

PO Box 510
Reedville, VA 22539
phone: (804) 453-4737
email: pfox@pfox.org
website: www.pfox.org

PFOX believes many gays wish to return to a straight lifestyle. The organization contends that sex education classes should advise gay students that heterosexuality is an option for them. By following the "Education/Schools" link on the PFOX website, students can find numerous studies, news articles, and opinion pieces in support of the group's philosophy.

Planned Parenthood Federation of America
434 W. Thirty-Third St.
New York, NY 10001
phone: (212) 541-7800
fax: (212) 245-1845
website: www.plannedparenthood.org

Planned Parenthood operates more than eight hundred clinics across the country, all of which provide contraceptive services to adolescent girls. The organization also maintains an active sex education program, providing educators and speakers for schools.

Sexuality Information and Education Council of the United States (SIECUS)
90 John St., Suite 402
New York, NY 10038
phone: (212) 819-9770
fax: (212) 819-9776
website: www.siecus.org

Founded in 1964, SIECUS was the first organization to design a sex education curriculum focusing on contraception. By following the link to "Policy and Advocacy" on the organization's website, students can find statistics on the effectiveness of abstinence-only and comprehensive sex ed programs as well as issues involving gay students.

Additional Reading

Books

Aine Collier, *The Humble Little Condom: A History*. New York: Prometheus, 2007.

Alesha Doan and Jean Calterone Williams, *The Politics of Virginity: Abstinence in Sex Education*. Westport, CT: Praeger, 2008.

Susan Kathleen Freeman, *Sex Goes to School: Girls and Sex Education Before the 1960s*. Champaign: University of Illinois Press, 2008.

Lisa Frohnapfel-Krueger, ed., *Teen Pregnancy and Parenting*. Farmington Hills, MI: Greenhaven, 2010.

Alexandra M. Lord, *Condom Nation: The U.S. Government's Sex Education Campaign from World War I to the Internet*. Baltimore: Johns Hopkins University Press, 2010.

Kristin Luker, *When Sex Goes to School: Warring Views on Sex—and Sex Education—Since the Sixties*. New York: W.W. Norton, 2006.

Olivia Picklesimer, ed., *Teen Sex*. Farmington Hills, MI: Greenhaven, 2010.

Alan Soble, *Sex from Plato to Paglia: A Philosophical Encyclopedia*. Westport, CT: Greenwood, 2006.

Periodicals

Jackie Alexander, "More Emphasis Needed on Preventing Teen Pregnancies, Officials Say," *Gainesville (FL) Sun*, March 13, 2012.

Amanda Gardner, "Teens' 'Unhealthy' Sex Exposure Blamed on TV, Music, Web," *USA Today*, September 6, 2011.

Landon Hall, "Abstinence Programs, Teen Pregnancy Linked?," *Orange County (CA) Register*, January 27, 2010.

Connie Schultz, "Parma High Schools Teens Make a Request for Real Sex Education," *Cleveland Plain Dealer*, February 24, 2010.

Bill Turque, "D.C. Schools Prepare for Nation's First Sex-Education Standardized Testing," *Washington Post*, September 14, 2011.

Internet Sources

Future of Sex Education, "The History of Sex Education." www.futureofsexed.org/background.html.

Mother Jones, "The Enemy in Your Pants: The Military's Decades-Long War Against STDs." http://motherjones.com/politics/2010/05/us-army-std/enemy-your-pants-9.

National Public Radio, "Sex Education in America: An NPR/Kaiser/Kennedy School Poll." www.npr.org/templates/story/story.php?storyId=1622610.

Pregnant Teen Help, "Teen Condom Use Statistics." www.pregnantteenhelp.org/statistics/teen-condom-use-statistics.

Index